NEW HOME SELLING STRATEGIES

The Professional's Handbook for Success

Nancy Davenport-Ennis

Real Estate
Education Company
a division of Dearborn Financial Publishing, Inc.

While a great deal of care has been taken to provide accurate and current information, the ideas, suggestions, general principles and conclusions presented in this book are subject to local, state and federal laws and regulations, court cases and any revisions of same. The reader is thus urged to consult legal counsel regarding any points of law—this publication should not be used as a substitute for competent legal advice.

Publisher: Kathleen A. Welton
Acquisitions Editor: Patrick J. Hogan
Associate Editor: Karen A. Christensen
Project Editor: Jack L. Kiburz
Cover Design: Mary Kushmir

© 1992 by NDE Impressions, Inc.
Published by Real Estate Education Company,
a division of Dearborn Financial Publishing, Inc.

Printed in the United States of America

92 93 94 10 9 8 7 6 5 4 3 2 1

Library of Congress Cataloging-in-Publication Data

Davenport-Ennis, Nancy.
    New home selling strategies : the professional's handbook for success / Nancy Davenport-Ennis.
        p.   cm.
    Includes index.
    ISBN 0-79310-354-1
    1. House selling. 2. Real estate business. I. Title.
HD1390.5.D38   1992   91-44234
    333.33'8—dc20   CIP

Contents

Exhibits

Introduction

The New Home Sales Industry is cyclical, complex and challenging. As we experience downward cycles in new home sales, the media, our association publications and even our peers frequently seem focused on the negative position of our industry. Headlines scream that we're down in new home starts, down in number of homes sold, down in available development and construction monies, and down in gross volume of sales. That's enough bad news to send even the most positive thinkers into fetal positions for an undetermined period of time! But wait—look at the upside of our marketplace.

Three fundamental positions remain constant:

- We have buyers who desire and buy new homes.

- We have builders who offer creatively designed products at affordable prices.

- We have financing available in this country so that anyone can enjoy the "great American dream" of home ownership.

If these positives exist in our market, why are those of us in sales and marketing feeling so lousy—or perhaps overchallenged? Maybe we've buried ourselves in the negatives and just need to climb out into the world of positives.

Counter the Negatives!

Specifically, those of us in new home sales must design strategies to counter the impact of the negatives . . .

If the media preaches rate instability, we should highlight the attractive pricing being offered by the builder, illustrating to the buyer that as the rates stabilize new home sales prices could increase.

When consumers challenge us to *sell* them on our product—we must *do it!* The key is to do it first by clarifying for the buyers *their three major priorities* in buying a home. Typically answers will involve pricing, terms, location, lifestyle features or design. If we know that these are the primary areas of comparison, it's our job to build an arsenal of "pluses" about each area of concern in order to overcome our purchasers' perception that our competition has more advantages.

Let's examine one possible situation: Your buyers want a new home priced between $180,000 and $185,000 and insist that their payments not exceed $1,600 per month. That's their main priority. They are quick to mention that your competitor is offering a reduced interest rate through a buydown that brings the payment to the desired $1,600. Your product would require a payment of $1,700 per month with no buydown available. Where do you go from here? To the positives:

- Your product has no homeowner association fees—the competitor's does ($60 per month).

- Your product offers a package of standard features that are not offered by the competitor, and to include these features in the competitor's product, the buyers must pay an additional $3,600 at closing. Amortize that amount over the proposed life of the loan and show that figure to the buyers, as well as the lost interest income on $3,600 cash. Help the buyers understand that either way—cash at closing or financing these items—they are making an additional investment in the home. Simply put, don't stop with monthly payments. Examine the full scope of monthly finances.

Back to Basics

It sounds simple, like the type of strategy we used when we were new in the business—the "back-to-basics approach." That's the answer! As well-trained, highly skilled professionals, we must get back to basics in our sales presentations. Even the most astute buyers in today's marketplace will base their buying decisions on the five basic areas of comparison mentioned previously.

We're told by the experts in our industry that the 1990s will position real estate salespeople in a service culture, and every customer will be looking for optimum service. Considering the time crunch we must work within, providing such service is a constant challenge. It's up to us to market ourselves and our products quickly, concisely, effectively and positively—beginning today!

Our marketplace has become a challenging arena where competition for available products, price incentives and qualified buyers is at an all-time high. As sales and marketing professionals, it's no longer acceptable to simply *love* what we do. We have to develop a passion for our business. A major component of that passion is self-directed motivation and excellence. It's our responsibility to immerse ourselves in positive actions, thoughts and people on a daily basis. Increased prospecting means an increased opportunity for sales results. And that's a positive action that only *we* can control!

Give yourself daily pep talks focused on defining objectives for the day and make them happen. Meet with successful new home salespeople—either in your market or outside your city—and share strategies on how to increase sales success in a sagging marketplace. Meet with relocation directors and give them your service package outlining the "kid glove" treatment you offer to every customer. Strive to attend every homebuilding and real estate industry meeting in your area to stay abreast of successful sales methods. These are simple steps, yes, but implementing them in a cyclical market means being prepared to swim upstream and challenge the negatives. Even in a cyclical market, there are four absolutes:

1. Buyers
2. Builders

3. Products

4. Available mortgage money

Your passion for positive performance on a daily basis is a must in the '90s. In this time of complexity, intense competition and overachievement, your personal commitment to excellence will result in professional services unequalled in your community. This book is designed to help you achieve excellence. Enjoy using this text as a reference for easy-to-follow procedures and simple solutions to everyday challenges in the new home sales business.

Your Career in New Home Sales

Have you ever taken the time to ask new home sales specialists what they do? The question elicits similar responses from many new home agents. "It's simple," they say:

> I have to do everything! Baby-sit the site! Stay on top of the construction schedule through the site superintendent! Put up with frequent interruptions from the subcontractors onsite who have learned one universal line well—"May I use the phone, please?"—delivered while they stand in your sparkling fresh model in their mud-laden boots! Tour the site with prospective purchasers and subsequently become their best friend, financial advisor (better known at times as a magician), psychologist and sales cheerleader all in the process of selling them a home and getting the contract to close! But let's not fail to mention that I'm also accountable to the builder for maintaining traffic, prospecting, closing and construction reports daily and to top it off, I'm the interior decorator making interior selections with each of our purchasers! Oops, one more hat for me to wear—I'm the marketing director, organizing REALTOR® events onsite, conducting direct mail campaigns and meeting with area advertisers to develop effective sales campaigns.

Are you tired after reading the agent's answer? If not, continue reading. What you'll discover is that the absolutely fascinating world of new home sales offers you an unlimited opportunity for personal growth and professional development, including refinement or complete development of management, sales, administrative, research and marketing skills. Your job in new home sales is multifaceted, and every facet brings with it an opportunity for growth through new challenges and innovative solutions.

What Is To Love and Not To Love About Selling New Homes?

Every job presents an opportunity for a love-hate cycle, because most jobs have processes to love and procedures to hate.

New home sales is not an exception. Answer the following two questions and then refer to Exhibit 1.1 on page 3 for some additional answers. Have fun with this; don't hold back!

What's To Love about New Home Selling?

1. _____
2. _____
3. _____
4. _____
5. _____
6. _____

What's Not To Love about Selling New Homes?

1. _____
2. _____
3. _____
4. _____
5. _____
6. _____

Exhibit 1.1   Selling New Homes: The Pros and Cons

> **What's To Love?!**
>
> - The product is beautiful.
> - You have one primary agent function—TO SELL.
> - You are a product expert.
> - You are a member of the elite when you're in new home selling within the real estate industry.
> - You dress up and typically spend the day in a beautiful model at a beautiful site.
> - You have a controlled sales position—same time daily, weekly, monthly: same product lines; same seller; same neighborhood.
>
> **What's Not To Love?!**
>
> - The builder is a bear!
> - The product is behind schedule—meaning delayed bucks to you.
> - Building trends can fluctuate dramatically having a direct impact on your income.
> - Buyers can be fickle—sometimes they're not too loyal!
> - There's too much product competition.

What Is Different about Selling New Homes?

The following customer and product information lists deal with what's different about selling new homes. Enjoy them and list any additional points you may have.

Your Customer

- They are frequently transferred families with an *urgency* to buy.

- They are often well-qualified transferees with the corporate financial support necessary to negotiate loan terms and provide immediate equity from the home they are leaving.

- They've been shopping comparatively in the market for approximately 19 months before buying.

- They're financially astute thanks to the media and often as a result of previous home ownership.

- They're very specific in their wants and needs—that's why they're buying NEW!

- They are typically qualified to buy.

Your Product

- New homes generally have efficient floor plans.

- New homes are clean and unused—no muss, no fuss!

- New homes generally appreciate more quickly than an existing house during the first few years of ownership.

- New homes are often sold with the builder.

- New homes require little or no maintenance or repair during the first few years.

- The buyer usually selects light fixtures, paint colors, floor coverings, wall coverings, etc.

- New homes generally have a better warranty program.

- There is no wait for a previous owner to move out.

- New homes usually offer attractive landscaping and curb appeal.

- New homes offer the newest in appliances and conveniences.

With consistent attention to the 80 percent emotional needs that all of your buyers have when you originate your sales presentations to them, you can be very successful in new home sales. It is your role as a new home sales specialist to consistently demonstrate rapport-building skills, product knowledge, financial expertise and attention to detail in the administrative cycle of prospecting, presentation, negotiating the contract and closing the sale.

The Site Agent Job Description

Just as no two people are exactly alike, no two home sites are exactly alike. If for no other reason, the mere fact that they are in two different physical locations makes them different. As you thoroughly review your job description, customize it to meet the needs of your site and your builder.

Review this description with your broker, sales managers, a new homes director and/or your builder, to develop an outline of responsibilities appropriate for your product, in your community, given your population and your competition.

Prospecting: Your Passage to Income Control

As an independent contractor, it is your responsibility to control your income through very specific prospecting programs—particularly when economic conditions shrink buyer segments. Repeatedly, the top sales award winners in real estate praise the merits of consistent, *daily* prospecting. Tom Hopkins, a nationally recognized sales trainer, stresses the importance of planned daily prospecting activities if you are to realize your financial goals.

Prospecting has long been recognized as a fundamental key to success in real estate resales. However, the new home sales marketplace historically assumed a passive prospecting posture in which agents expected their signage, model complexes, media coverage and builder product and incentives to *attract* buyers. Once buyers presented themselves at the site, agents were eager to make that sale! There's a major problem in this approach: if you only service the people who appear on the site you are passive in controlling your income.

In order to control your business growth and income, you must take *active* control of the prospecting function every day. Consider the old adage, "Nothing happens until you make a sale!" It's a bit like the pig in the garden. Though blind, even he roots up a potato occasionally! If you're relying on the passive prospecting discussed earlier, you're first cousins to our blind pig . . . and you simply get lucky when a prospect shows up.

Develop a prospecting plan of action for yourself in which you record on a calendar the specific time each day that you will devote to prospecting and the type of prospecting you'll be doing. Remember—a variety of methods affords a greater opportunity to capture a prospect. Review the prospecting suggestions that follow and incorporate as many as possible into your daily plan. Track your success monthly, and as you refine the methods that give you the greatest results, concentrate in those areas.

I commit to do the following prospecting activities:

■ Place outbound telephone prospecting calls daily to attract prospective buyers.   Goal: ____ calls per day.

- Knock on doors in the community and invite prospects to the model.

- Sponsor, coordinate and implement frequent events at the model home to reach potential buying prospects and co-broke agents.

- Schedule frequent direct mail campaigns to targeted groups of potential buyers.

- Track daily prospects who visit the model home. See Exhibit 1.2 on page 7 for a suggested Guest Comment card format.

- Follow up with every visitor to the model home and every prospect gained through phone and door-knocking activities. Mail a note to visitors within 24 hours of their visit.

Specific follow-up should include:

- A written note mailed within 24 hours of your first contact with a prospect. (See Exhibit 1.3 for a sample follow-up letter.)

- A phone follow-up with the prospect within five days of initial contact. (Record the date, type of call and future work required.)

- A weekly follow-up call or note until the prospects BUY and CLOSE their sale. When someone has been deleted as a buying prospect, record this on the tracking form where requested.

Prepare handouts to include:

- Preparation of a Competitive Market Analysis (CMA) of competitive properties within a five-mile radius of the site. The site agent is to complete a subdivision profile of competing properties and keep a copy onsite and a copy on file in the New Homes Department. These profiles are to be updated every quarter to be shared with prospects.

- A primary brochure of the community to be shared with prospects who exhibit a willingness to buy and are financially qualified to do so. This brochure typically contains detailed verbal and visual descriptions of the community.

- A secondary brochure to be shared with all prospects that highlights community features in a modified, less expensive format.

Exhibit 1.2   Guest Registration and Comments

Name _____

Address _____

City/State _____ Zip _____

Home# _____ Work# _____

Our marketing department would like to know how you heard about us:

___ TV Channel _____

___ Newspaper (name) _____

___ Magazine (name) _____

___ Radio (station name) _____

___ Direct Mail (date) _____

___ Friend (name) _____

___ Driving By _____

___ Brochure _____

___ REALTOR® (name) _____

___ Realty Company _____

Type of home desired: ___ Apartment   ___ Townhome

                          ___ Condo   ___ Single Family

Date needed _____

Number to live in household _____

I presently: ___ own   ___ rent   ___ lease   ___ other

My age group is:

___ under 25   ___ 25-35   ___ 36-45   ___ 46-55   ___56-65   ___over 65

My employment is: ___ civilian   ___self-employed   ___ military   ___ retired

Price range desired _____

My yearly income is: ___ up to 20,000   ___ 21,000-30,000   ___ 31,000-40,000

                       ___ 41,000-50,000   ___ 51,000-59,000   ___ over 60,000

Visitor comments: _____

_____

_____

I need occupancy in: ___ 6 weeks ___ 3 months ___ 6 months ___ other

---

Exhibit 1.3   Sample Letter

Follow-Up Letter after Prospect's Second Visit

```
Dear _____,

Thank you for your continued interest in (name of development). We hope you enjoyed
your recent visit with us; it was a pleasure to see you again.
We take pride in what we do. Our commitment to excellence and attention to detail set us
apart in a competitive market. Quality housing requires superior craftsmanship, comfort-
able surroundings and people who care. We provide this and more.
Once again, we appreciate your interest in our community and hope to be of service to
you. Please call when we can be of further assistance!
                              Sincerely,
```

Tracking and Capturing the "Be-Back" Business

In today's market, the average new home buyer stays in the market one year before making a buying decision, visits 13 homes and returns four times to the ultimate site he or she desires to purchase before negotiating a contract. Can you see how easy it would be to lose this prospect? What can you do to avoid such a loss?

Consistent commitment to good record-keeping in new home sales is the first step toward capturing the be-back market. This begins by having every visitor complete a guest registration card which will be discussed in further detail in Chapter 4. Please refer to Exhibit 1.4 on page 14 and note the Be-Back Tracking Form that is a part of your original guest registration card. If you program this form into your computer, it will allow you to establish one file per prospect. If you're into manual tracking, this form saves hassles both in data collections and filing.

To have be-backs, you must, within your job responsibility, handle the following services with skill and sensitivity to the prospect. Let's review!

"Nothing happens till someone sells a house." This often involves:

- Showing the property and its hidden values

- Asking qualifying questions and *listening* for buying signals

- Pre-qualifying prospects

- Becoming knowledgeable about financing
- Closing the sale—being able to get it on paper
- Advising on loan application and follow-up
- Coordinating purchaser selections in a timely manner
- Meeting with the appraiser and providing backup information
- Recommending closing attorneys and attending all closings
- Arranging and attending walk-thrus and coordinating onsite schedules with superintendent
- Inspecting the site weekly to determine construction status and to catch errors that may arise
- Coordinating all necessary information with the attorneys and loan company for a smooth settlement
- Collecting the closing check

Presenting Against the Competition

All buyers want a "deal"—something to convince themselves, their families and their friends that they've made a wise choice. It's your job to supply sufficient research data convincing your buyers that they have made the best buying decision. Include the following in your presentation:

- The convenience, beauty, prestige and/or investment advantages of this location
- Price support through a Competitive Market Analysis that favorably positions your property in the market in terms of present homes sold, amenities included, terms of sale and pricing
- A review of the home warranty to allay fears of future maintenance
- A meeting with the builder or his or her representative if persistent questions relating to construction remain a point of concern. Be certain that you profile the *pluses* of your construction that might include soundproofing, structural reinforcement and heavy insulation using product names that stimulate consumer confidence if they are names that will be recognized.

Remember, your job is to present the facts that position your product competitively in the marketplace.

Communicating Through Follow-Up Channels and Systems

Weekly subdivision reports to the broker, builders, co-broke agent and buyer keep everyone on track. These reports, samples of which are discussed in detail in Chapter 8, include the following:

- Builder Authorization Form
- Referral Form
- Weekly Prospecting Report
- New Homes Product Input Report
- Site Consultant Prospecting Log
- Open Contract Tracking Form
- Financial Information Report
- Loan Status Reports
- Construction Status Reports
- Closing Reports
- Weekly Traffic Report

Maintaining the Site

Your site has a lot in common with you—it has only one opportunity to make a powerful first impression. Help it along by doing the following:

- Ensure proper watering.
- Sweep walkways.
- Police your sales office:
  - Organize your desk.
  - Pre-assemble your brochures.
  - Have contracts available and ready for action.
  - Keep your refreshment area tidy.
  - Maintain the plat (sales map).
  - Update renderings and floor plans.
  - Keep displays, walls and carpet clean.

- Organize your files.
- Empty wastebaskets.
- Keep decorator selection samples intact.

■ Signage responsibilities:

- Straighten and/or replace damaged signs.
- Police the silent salespersons—your directional, entry and informational signs.
- Keep the builder informed of sign inventory.
- Be alert for shopworn billboards or directional signs and notify the appropriate party to replace or repair them.

Providing Product Feedback to the Builder

Builders have only one way of learning how prospective buyers respond to their product, community design and amenities—from you, the New Home Sales Specialist! In Chapter 8, builder meetings will be discussed in detail, but here is a brief review of the feedback you should be providing to the builder:

■ What are the most popular models and why?

■ Is there an unbalanced inventory? Are there too many products of one type, such as multi-family with one bedroom and not enough of a more desired product?

■ What do the consumers prefer? (The likes and dislikes listed on the Aye/Nay Sheets)

(Refer to Exhibits in Chapter 8.)

■ What options have been included?

■ What are the punch list item problems?

■ Have there been service breakdowns?

Advertising and Marketing Requirements

You meet the buyers of your product daily. You know them demographically and can list their hot buttons regarding the product, amenities, sales incentives and site development. Help your marketing representative tell the world all that you know about your buyer segments and do the following regularly:

■ Maintain an advertising/publicity scrapbook.

■ Know which ad pulled best and why. (Report this to the agency.)

■ Select houses to feature in future ads.

■ Use unusual selling propositions that emphasize the unique pluses of the property.

■ Make copy suggestions.

■ Track the demographics of your prospects and buyers.

■ Read your ads and the competition's daily.

Improving Yourself

Nothing grows without nurturing. As a new home sales specialist, carefully review the following list of personal growth steps that could nurture your professional growth and positive attitude:

■ Read *Builder* and *Professional Builder* every month.

■ Keep your automobile clean.

■ Practice good grooming habits.

■ Attend national and local Sales and Marketing Council functions.

■ Read one new book on selling each month.

■ Know your competition.

■ Constantly update your product knowledge.

■ Set goals for self-motivation.

■ Read industry magazines for decorating trends and terminology.

■ Know how to operate every appliance in your homes.

■ Keep a notebook of questions you cannot answer; get the answers.

■ Stay in shape physically and mentally.

Servicing the Sale after the Closing

Your fundamental responsibilities after the sale are identified below:

- Be a liaison with servicemen on punch list items to assure your client that they will be done.

- Ramrod complaints and demand results from the builder.

- Supply your buyers with assistance on move-in day and into the first week after moving. Provide lists of emergency phone numbers and carry-in food service menus with phone numbers. For families with young children, offer to coordinate child care with an area day care center.

- Be available after move-in day to answer questions and reaffirm the good decision your buyer has made.

- Deliver a housewarming gift within 30 days of move-in.

Now that you've reviewed this master list of job responsibilities, answer this question: "What's my job at my site with my builder?" Remember, you're in the most competitive area of real estate when you're in new home sales, so reach for the opportunities and develop a concise job description.

Exhibit 1.4   "Be-Back" Tracking and Follow-Up Form

BE-BACK TRACKING FORM

Date _____

Agent _____

Was prospect shown to a property?   _____ yes   _____ no

If No, Reason _____

If Yes, which Property(s) _____

_____

_____

FOLLOW-UP

Date Thank You Note Sent _____

Phone Calls

1st Date: _____   Results_____

2nd Date: _____   Results_____

3rd Date: _____   Results_____

Be-Back Appointments: _____

_____

_____

Comments: _____

_____

_____

The Foundation for Success: Understanding Yourself and Your Market

Information is power. By selecting this book, you have already shown an interest in improving yourself through education. Your success in new home selling is based first on an understanding of your strengths and weaknesses as a salesperson, and secondly, an understanding of who your buyer is. This chapter will start you on the road to self-evaluation and then outline specific demographic information that defines your marketplace.

Take a Look at Yourself

In order to reach any new horizon in personal and professional growth, it is necessary to continually assess where your attitudes and behaviors are while tracking the positive and negative trends in each area. The following tests are designed to do that for you.

There are no right or wrong answers. Simply review your answers to track trends. If the trend is negative, program changes into your daily behaviors and attitudes. If the trends are positive, pat yourself on the back—and keep practicing the positive behaviors and attitudes!

Self-Evaluation Test for New Homes Salespersons

Name _____   Date _____

Speech

1. Do you talk monotonously? _____

2. Do you enunciate your words clearly? _____

3. Do you speak with enthusiasm and conviction? _____

4. Do you use power language? _____

5. Have you mastered the use of architect, builder and owner talk?

    _____

Impression

1. Do you make a good impression from the following standpoints?

    a. Approach _____

    b. Physique _____

    c. Posture _____

    d. Clothing _____

    e. Facial Expression _____

2. Do you leave as favorable an impression at the end of your interview as you made at the beginning? _____

3. Do you project sincerity and honesty? _____

Steady Application

1. Do you keep your energy at a high level throughout the day, especially in the latter part of the afternoon? _____

2. Do you get started early after breakfast and after lunch? _____

3. Do you take too much time for your midday meal? _____

4. Do you continue working right up until dark? _____

5. Do you work steadily day after day? _____

6. Do you note buyer resistances you can't overcome and ask advice?

_____

7. To sum it up, have you the vitality (the opposite of laziness) necessary to be successful? _____

Perseverance

1. Do you stay with the prospect as long as there is the slightest possibility of closing? _____

2. Do you handle objections intelligently? _____

3. If, when you attempt to close, you are turned down once, do you give up or do you make repeated attempts? _____

4. Do you try to close a number of times on the first tour? _____

5. Do you lose your enthusiasm after two or three prospects have turned you down? _____

6. Do you have the stamina/persistence to be a successful salesperson?

_____

Self-Management

1. Do you continually plan to secure new prospects? _____

2. Do you make an effort, through friends, acquaintances and others to meet new prospects? _____

3. Do you systematically make an effort to improve your sales talk?

_____

4. Do you read and study to increase your knowledge? _____

5. Do you analyze yourself periodically and improve weak points? ___

Tact

1. Do you always keep your temper? _____

2. Are you always courteous? _____

3. Do you make your presentation from the prospect's viewpoint or do you think only of making a sale? _____

4.   Do you know your competition and are you prepared to meet it?

_____

Loyalty

1.   Do you faithfully follow instructions? _____

2.   Can you stand fair criticism? _____

3.   Do you always boost your organization? _____

4.   Are you loyal to your manager and/or builder? _____

5.   Do you work on good terms with other salespeople? _____

Resourcefulness

1.   Do you succeed in communicating with difficult prospects? _____

2.   Are you successful at handling objections? _____

3.   Do you try to implement your own new selling ideas? _____

4.   Do you follow your manager's suggestions regarding selling?

_____

5.   Are you able to self-motivate when a prospect turns you down?

_____

6.   Do you objectively analyze your successes and failures? _____

7.   Do you try to improve your selling presentation after a "no sale"?

_____

8.   Do you demonstrate your homes on a continuing basis? _____

9.   Are you professional in getting your prospects emotionally involved?

_____

Observation

1.   Do you vary your sales presentation with different prospects?

_____

2. Do your remarks indicate that you carefully observe each prospect and fit your sales talk to their buyer type, buying stages and dominant buying motive? _____

3. Do you go to the trouble of deep-qualifying your prospect before you begin closing? _____

4. Do you exaggerate? _____

5. Do you understand your competition? _____

6. Do you know your construction and how all home appliances work?
   _____

7. Do you treat your competitors fairly? _____

8. Do you know your community? _____

9. Do you know all aspects of your financing? _____

Sociability

1. Are you steadily enlarging your circle of acquaintances? _____

2. Do you attend lodge and club meetings, Chamber of Commerce meetings, community betterment affairs and the like? _____

Appearance

1. Do you make a pleasing impression? _____

2. Are your clothes in good taste? _____

3. Are your clothes well-pressed; your collars clean and shoes shined?
   _____

Health

1. Do you recognize that good health is an asset? _____

2. Do you eat too much? _____

3. Do you drink too much? _____

4. Do you smoke? _____

5. Are you easily tired? _____

Orderliness

1. Do you go to great lengths to get the names, addresses and phone numbers of all prospects? _____

2. Do you keep *personal* records of prospect names, addresses and phone numbers? _____

3. Do you make your call-backs systematically? _____

4. Do you set aside a certain time for telephone follow-up each week?

    _____

5. Are you prompt in keeping appointments? _____

6. Do you complete reports for management in an orderly fashion?

    _____

Sales Technique

1. Do you approach and warm up professionally? _____

2. Do you know how to quick-qualify in a high traffic situation?

    _____

3. In warming up the prospect's attention into interest, do you bring the prospects into the picture—do you show them how they will profit by purchasing your home? _____

4. Do you convince the prospect that investing in your new home is a sensible thing to do? _____

5. Do you close with strength, firmness and some knowledge of the fine art of closing? _____

6. Do you use "trial closings"? _____

7. Is your sales talk too involved? _____

8. Do you try to tell the entire story and thus draw it out too long?

    _____

9. Do you know when to "shut up" and start writing? _____

10. Do you remain in the closing posture and keep closing or do you give up too quickly? _____

11. Do you stay aware of objections and keep neutralizing them?

    _____

12. Do you realize that a sale is made when you give the prospect one more close than the objections they give you? _____

13. Do you become deeply involved in the post-sale selling process?

_____

Self-Analysis of Telephone Selling Skills

For Preparation	**Yes**	**No**
Did I have ads, lists, numbers ready for telephoning?	__	__
Did I have paper, pencils, calendar, materials ready?	__	__
Did I know exactly what I was going to say?	__	__
Did I have answers ready for common objections?	__	__
Did I have the attitude that I would obtain the appointment?	__	__

For Technique

Did I know the prospect's name?	__	__
Did I make his/her name important in the interview?	__	__
Did I listen to the prospect's voice, vocabulary and needs?	__	__
Did I repeat points in which he/she expressed an interest?	__	__
Did I show an interest in him/her?	__	__
Was I careful not to interrupt?	__	__

For Prospect's Interest

Did I use "sizzle" to gain attention?	__	__
Did I inspire confidence by being sincere and enthusiastic?	__	__
Did I project my voice and transmit my personality?	__	__
Did I use short, vivid, descriptive picture words?	__	__

Did I stick to the presentation in a concise, logical order?   ___ ___

Was my presentation to do something "for" not "to"
the prospect?   ___ ___

For Empathy

Did I avoid arguments and signs of pressure?   ___ ___

Did I avoid an apologetic manner or timidity?   ___ ___

Did I speak with firmness and authority?   ___ ___

Did I smile and retain a level, courteous tone?   ___ ___

Did I build the prospect's ego rather than talk down?   ___ ___

Was I aware of the proper time to call the prospect?   ___ ___

For Professionalism

Did I "telegraph" my message?   ___ ___

Did I have a "hinge" on which to hang my conversation?   ___ ___

Did I give the prospect a "benefit" from listening to me?   ___ ___

Did I maintain a "customer you" attitude?   ___ ___

Did I offer the prospect a choice?   ___ ___

Did I answer every objection intelligently?   ___ ___

Did I keep the appointment my sole objective?   ___ ___

Did I prevent the prospect from giving a definite "no"?   ___ ___

Did I ask for the appointment instead of hinting at it?   ___ ___

Was my interview conducted in a professional manner?   ___ ___

The Facts about Your Marketplace

As specialists, new home salespersons are committed to mastering and constantly updating a battery of specific product, financial and competitor information that serves to position them and their products as front-runners in the eyes of their prospects and their builders. It is essential to assemble detailed data about the marketplace itself. It is difficult to sell any product without thoroughly understanding fundamentals—the socio-economic characteristics of today's buyer and seller and the demanded services and goods.

To reach your sales goals, it's best to know what the employment and per capita income figures are within your community in order to frame a snapshot of the economic well-being of your marketplace. Many sales-people are committed to the concept that they'll reach their goals in spite of their market condition and there's validity in that attitude. It is, however, easier to hit a *known* stationary target than an ill-defined moving one.

The greatest resources for information that helps you understand your marketplace are your local Chamber of Commerce, unemployment and building permits offices, the state Labor Department and the courthouse that records all local closings or property transfers. From these primary sources, you can examine population trends in your market, median household income, per capita income, an analysis of the labor force in terms of actual unemployment figures and area employment trends. You can also review the number of building permits issued versus the number of actual new homes closing by product in your marketplace.

Population

Population trends in any given area establish the types of services, goods, recreational, cultural and employment opportunities that are either present today or being planned for tomorrow. As a new home specialist, once you define the primary segments in your population base, it becomes easy to identify the types, sizes and prices of housing that are needed. As an example, if your population base is principally 30 to 38 years of age; married with children *at home*; dual income parents who are middle management employees, the product prescribed for this segment is neither a one-bedroom townhouse with a studio loft nor a move-up luxury home priced at the high end of the market.

The more thoroughly you can understand your population both demographically—in terms of income, age, marital and familial status—and psychographically—in terms of their intrinsic motivators (what they love in their lifestyle)—the more effective your sales and product presentation will be. As you skillfully define and understand your buyer markets, you will avoid representing products for which there is no clearly defined market. This simple strategy moves you one step closer to attaining excellence in achieving your personal sales goals through serving a base of satisfied customers.

Median Household Income

Defining median household income affords you the necessary data to target "affordable housing" within your community. Income levels, which vary greatly by area of the country, dictate the discretionary spending preferences of the population and that includes housing expenses. Median income information allows you to readily define the upper or lower income purchasers for your area. For example, a purchaser with a median household income of $50,500 per year would be an *upper income purchaser* in Gloucester County, Virginia. That same purchaser would be a *lower income purchaser* in Darien, Connecticut, where the per capita income exceeds $25,500 per year. When you understand income strata, you can define products within your community, city and/or county that are affordable, bargains or luxury homes for your population.

Analysis of the Labor Force

Home styles, amenity packages, lot designs and size and product mix within any city are defined by the demographics of the population. The labor force analysis reveals the percentage of persons within your community who are industrial employees, corporate executives, middle management personnel, physicians, support personnel, teachers, military, retirees, farm laborers and service personnel. As these labor groups are clearly identified, you as a sales specialist can target your marketing campaigns to effectively reach the buyer groups you need for your particular products. You can also define geographic locations that would be desirable for new products with easy access for strong segments of your labor force.

Employment Rate

Not only is it critical that you know the principal labor forces within your area, you must also track employment trends. This information is supplied by your state Labor Department and frequently by your Chamber of Commerce. If you define a steady trend of upward growth through the development of corporate centers or industrial complexes, military base expansions or simply the creation of new job opportunities within your area, it is a strong indicator that new home construction and sales will remain steady within your market.

Home starts are tied directly to new job openings so REALTORS® who consistently check the pulse of new jobs within their market will have a distinct advantage in knowing when to promote new construction products and when to close out current projects.

You have the responsibility to know your marketplace and understand the overwhelming impact—both positive and negative—that can be experienced in your sales profession.

As you take the plunge into researching your marketplace, the following quotes might brighten your work.

"When things go wrong, don't go with them." (Anonymous)

"It's easier to do a job right than to explain why you didn't."

Learning the facts about your marketplace adds to your credibility as a specialist in the eyes of your prospects, buyers and builder/developer clients and builds the self-confidence that allows you to function successfully within your marketplace.

3

Understanding the Builder: Community Concepts, Proposed Buyer Groups and Expectations

A successful team identifies mutual expectations and common goals. In the Builder/Developer—Salesperson team, the salesperson must understand the builder's product, community concepts, targeted buyer groups, sales and prospecting performance goals and ratios if he or she is to achieve the sales success needed by the lender to meet pro forma requirements. The salesperson is also expected by the builder to meet production deadlines and achieve profit margins based on timely sales of the product.

To define these mutual expectations and common goals, the following *Initial Interviewing Questions* should be used. Make an appointment with the builder and ask for about an hour of time. Remember that time is the builder's most precious commodity, so once the one-hour meeting has been agreed to, control your time by using a streamlined agenda of questions.

Experience has shown repeatedly that these questions move builders into their comfort zones—talking about their professional love, their community, their product and their personal sales expectations. You become a hero to the builder when you provide a platform that allows them to share specific insights and product observations about their project. You enter their world on their terms instead of arriving in the office carrying the age-old sales mantel that proclaims "I'm the biggest and best company and agent in town."

27

The complexities of today's new home sales market demand a thorough understanding of every project from the master plan analysis to the product profile to the builder's sales needs and personal requirements. These questions give you the insight needed to evaluate what sales services will be required to sell this product and to determine if the product, buyer profile and sales expectations are realistic within your given marketplace.

Defining the Builder's Community Concepts

Product Type

Ask the builder to define the product in terms of type (single family, townhouses, condominiums) and style (contemporary, traditional, transitional). Ask about the proposed room arrangement, volume features such as vaulted ceilings, dramatic multi-story windows, etc., and consumer pluses including standard upgraded features such as skylights or special mouldings, standard built-ins such as closet storage, drawers or shelves, bookcases, kitchen appliances, garages and bonus storage areas.

Community Theme

Ask the builder to identify the primary marketing theme that will be used in all promotional materials. These themes will typically center around one of the following topics:

- Location (Prestige, convenience, security)

- Affordability (Initial or long-term investment features)

- Snob Appeal (Better known as the "Prestige Factor")

- Comfort—typically this theme develops around privacy, luxury in kitchen, baths or entertaining areas, versatile development of space for large families with active young children and teens and outdoor or community amenities such as patios, porches, decks, pools, clubhouse, tennis courts, etc.

- The Love Factor—this theme builds on the dominant feature that the majority of all targeted buyers will love such as:

  - golf course location

- waterfront

- mountain view

- fireplace

- gourmet kitchen

- complete social center at home—Clubhouse/Recreational complex

Once the builder has identified the community theme for you, it's your job to determine whether the theme parallels your concept of what's most appealing to the lifestyle of the primary buyer. Since the primary buyer's interest is affordability, that must be discussed with your builder. You must have confidence in the theme in order to support the mutual expectations that it will effectively promote your product.

Planned Entry Graphics

Ask the builder to show you a layout of the design for the entry including fencing, signage, lighting plan and landscape design. Remember, the community has only one opportunity to make a good first impression and that begins with the entry.

Planned Site Amenities

Have the builder show you or discuss with you the master plan of the community. It's best to review the drawings that reflect common green areas, traffic and parking patterns, community lighting design and the site amenities. Your objective is to confirm that the amenities will be developed as part of a well-designed, balanced feature for the neighborhood. Obvious site amenities include pools, clubhouses, tennis courts, racquetball courts (outdoors), exercise spas, jogging, biking and walking trails, passive parks, children's play areas and pet exercise centers. The list goes on depending upon your buyer profile and geographic location.

In discussing the amenities, also define the following:

■ When will these amenities be built? At this point, you're trying to define a schedule of construction that enhances the sales program. Remember that the adage "Seeing is believing" is never truer than today when a consumer fears that the site amenities may never be built. It is quite feasible for the builder or developer to build some of the amenities in stages compatible with the development of new sections within the community. The most desired format is one in which the "cameo" amenity of the community is built as the initial site development and product construction is begun for Phase I of a multi-phased site.

Special Financing Incentives

Ask the builder about financial programs. To infuse a strong sales momentum in a new community, builders and lenders frequently cooperate to offer an initial package of attractive financial incentives. The following list represents a few of the incentives commonly used by builders.

■ Buydown mortgage rates

■ A certain number of points paid by the builder per loan

■ Builder reimbursement of those points as a cash discount to a purchaser who is paying cash or using a conventional loan

■ Bonus incentives at the time of pre-sell or closeout sales campaigns. Determine if appliance packages, carpet or light upgrades, luxury features such as bathroom sauna or outdoor jacuzzi may be offered in these campaigns. Contrast and compare this to what the competition is doing and see where your incentives stand.

■ Commission incentives to selling agents

■ Bonus packages to selling agents such as trips or personal gifts

■ Closing costs. Have the builder be very specific in identifying every closing cost to be paid and evaluate this to determine if these closing costs will effectively compete in your market.

Defining the Proposed Buyer Market

Social Profile

Ask builders to tell you what they think buyers's daily lifestyles are like, what they love in their homes, their neighborhood and adjacent community. This profile helps you *feel* who these buyers are and what they enjoy about life—including their hobbies, leisure time activities and daily lifestyle in terms of work and entertainment of family and friends both at home and in the community. This profile also reflects the cultural, recreational, educational and social preferences of family members. The better we understand this profile, the more completely we can design a sales and marketing campaign to attract and keep our buyer's attention.

Primary Market

Primary Market simply refers to the primary buyer for this neighborhood. New-home communities include a myriad of purchasers, but one primary buyer type usually emerges. These can include, but are not limited to, any of the following broad generalizations of buyer groups:

- *Singles*—Young, senior or single again

- *Mingles*—Unmarried couples

- *Yuppies*—The stereotypical college graduate conservatives focused on career development and the acquisition of material goods; symbols of success are of critical importance to this buyer group.

- *Dinks*—"Double Income No Kids" Buyers

- *Empty Nesters*—Older married couples whose children have grown and left home; they may desire a move down in space but frequently a move up in quality and comfort.

- *Retirees*—Older adults who have retired from their jobs. It is important to differentiate between the active retiree who travels, plays golf, exercises and entertains from the more senior retiree who enjoys quiet reflection, reading and family-focused activities. These two retiree groups demand very different home products and amenities.

- *Move-up Buyers*—Frequently this is a family with children looking for a larger home.

- *First Time Buyers*—Singles, singles again buying for the first time or newlyweds

- *Investor Buyers*—These individuals buy and sell real estate consistently to build investment portfolios and capital.

Also ask the builder to identify the secondary layers of buyers projected to purchase in the neighborhood. You can then evaluate the compatibility of the proposed master plan, product type and pricing with the buyer markets. If you have a match, your sales objectives have a higher degree of success. If your professional expertise and experience tell you there is a mismatch with any of the identified factors, discuss this with the builder and determine a corrective strategy to map a path to success.

Defining the Builder's Sales Expectations

Absorption Rate Versus Lender Pro Forma Requirements

Be sure you have a clear understanding of your builder's expectations. Builders have goals of how many homes should sell per month that are influenced by their personal desire to achieve a desired profit margin in a *timely* sales program. The builder frequently identifies an aggressive sales number per month allowing for a fallout ratio of contracts written versus contracts closed as well as an allowance for inconsistent sales performance. Builders have too frequently observed agents who sell sporadically— they're hot while they're hot but then when their personal financial goals have been met, their sales activity cools down. Unfortunately, the builder has a clock ticking daily that necessitates the kind of consistent sales activity that results in the sale of a desired number of products annually.

It's also important to identify the *minimum* number of sales required by the bank per month within the builder's pro forma (a job analysis prepared for the lender showing proposed construction costs and proposed sales analysis per year). The lender will base future renewals of the construction line of credit on that sales pro forma. Your job is to work daily to achieve those necessary sales results—that's job security for both you and the builder. You become the builder's ally in meeting the demands of the lending institution.

Average Percentage of Sales Price Versus Contract Price Expected

Every marketplace defines sales price. Historically, a few specialized areas such as resort markets, consistently show that the listed price is the sold price. Economic trends will affect the inventory of new homes. At this writing, with the impact of recessionary trends throughout this country and the reduction in corporate and military relocation business, the margin between list price and sales price has widened. Check with your local Home Builders Association to confirm their tracking of list prices versus sold prices within your market. If they do not have these records, ask them for a reference to a local statistician who may offer this research information in a monthly report. Also, your local Multiple Listing Service would have numbers reflective of both new home and resale activity.

Your objective is to determine what the builder expects in sales price versus contract price and then to check expectations against the market norm. For example, if the market consistently shows a four percent difference between list and contract price, check to see if the builder's expectations are within that normal range.

Builder Expectations

Every builder has specific sales expectations typically based on a series of prospecting, presentation, written contracts and closing expectations. Ask the following questions so you'll know the expectations that comprise the foundation of your job description if you sell this product.

Registered Guests Ratio to Contracts Written The National Association of Home Builders annually publishes a summary reference of the national norm concerning many aspects of new home sales and construction. One consistent statistic indicates that for every 10 visitors, one resulting contract should be written. This statistic is influenced by your ability to get *qualified* buyers to the site and not just lookers. It is important that you know what your builder expects in this regard.

Prospecting Systems: Active Versus Passive

Ask what level of prospecting the builder expects. The more sophisticated and experienced the builder, the more likely the requirement that you provide active prospecting support to your job description.

Passive Prospecting is any prospecting that does not require day-to-day support and follow-up by the agent to produce prospects. Examples would be offsite signage including billboards, onsite signage, print ads, radio and television commercials, direct-mail campaigns and brochures. Although each of these may involve the agent in planning, once completed agent involvement becomes secondary, or passive, requiring only follow-up with a prospect originated by one of these passive prospecting sources.

Active Prospecting demands daily involvement by the agent in *personally* striving to get a prospect to come to the site to make a buying decision. The following active prospecting methods apply:

- *Telephone Prospecting*—a very simple, effective technique. You call a specific number of prospects daily to invite them to your site. Ideally calls are targeted to a particular area that might generate substantial results in active prospects.

- *Personal presentations* weekly to social, civic or business organizations (such as local real estate companies) promoting your community. A videotape presentation of your community followed by the distribution of brochures or handouts can be very effective and provide an excellent network of new prospects.

- *Agent co-broke events* onsite; this may include lunch after a sales meeting and site tour.

- *Daily mail campaigns* in which you send a specific number of invitations each day inviting people to come to your site and follow up with them by phone.

- *Events onsite monthly* for prospective purchasers; these may include a home buyers seminar, decorating, patio planting, child safety and lawn care seminars geared to attract potential purchasers to the site.

Active prospecting helps secure your position with the builder when sales become sluggish. The builder can easily evaluate your performance in consistently prospecting to generate buyers to the site and can feel encouraged that your active prospecting supports his or her passive campaigns. Be certain to ask specifically how many active prospecting activities or contacts the builder requires per week and build your program accordingly.

Please refer to Exhibit 3.1, *Initial Interviewing Questions*, for a personal questionnaire outline ready to copy and implement in the field today.

Exhibit 3.1   Initial Interviewing Questions

These questions are to be used to interview the builder in order to have a clear picture of what the sales goals must be and who the target markets are. Seek definitive responses that will clarify if the builder is on target with absorption/performance goals, a perception of who the buyers are and a proposal of amenities and initial impact programs as they relate to competitive positioning in your market:

1.   Product Type

2.   Community Theme

3.   Planned Entry Graphics

4.   Planned Site Amenities

5.   Special Financing Incentives

6.   Absorption Rate Versus Lender Pro Forma Requirements

7.   Defining the Proposed Buyer Market

- Social Profile of Buyer

- Primary Market

- Secondary Market

8.   Defining the Builder's Expectations of Sales Performance

- Registered Guests Ratio to Contracts

- Average Percentage of Sales Price Versus Contract Price Expected

- Prospecting Systems Required: Active Versus Passive

The First Essential Steps To Selling New Homes: Greeting and Qualifying

As you strive to excel in new home sales, it is imperative to practice the basics of good salesmanship. The five essential steps of selling give you firm direction on how to handle the greeting, qualifying, demonstrating, becoming a financing expert and closing that are the basics of new home sales. This chapter focuses on greeting and qualifying prospects; the next three chapters outline the process.

The *greeting* is without a doubt the single most important step to accomplish in order to be successful in sales. This book profiles every concrete behavior you'll need to implement in order to build rapport with your customers. Both verbal and nonverbal communication are examined and discussed in detail in this chapter. The two universal communication styles are also discussed in depth in an effort to teach you how to effectively question both communicators. Spend quality time with this section of the chapter to considerably enhance your sales skills.

Qualifying is the age-old dilemma—or demon—as some might say. You need to know financial information about a family, but you don't want to offend your customer—or embarrass yourself. Throughout this section of Chapter 4, there is one objective: ***To make qualifying a comfortable process for all.***

You will find specific instructions and strategies to make your qualifying less painful and more successful. Additionally, sample questions and the order in which to ask them are provided and explained. If qualifying is an Achilles' heel for you, study this chapter in order to acquire beneficial methods for future use.

Step 1: The Greeting—The Once in a Lifetime Opportunity

Alfred Zunin, in his book *The First Four Minute Contact*, vividly reveals the powerful exchange of verbal and nonverbal data that occurs during an initial meeting. In the first four minutes of contact, you establish the boundaries that last the entire life of that future relationship. You make value judgments on what you do and don't like about a person, and what you do and don't trust in a person. As a sales specialist, your primary responsibility is to establish rapport with every prospect. You are trained to incorporate specific strategies in your day to day world to make that happen. For instance, consider the following five specific strategies.

1. *Buyers enter your homes with all senses on high.*

   ■ Check home odors and make sure the fragrances are pleasant such as potpourri or apple pie!

   ■ No smoking please in any of your models since many people object to smoke.

2. *Transmit warmth—Set the mood: lighting, sounds.*

   Use lamps to soften your lighting and add emphasis to your showing by turning on overhead lights as you move from room to room. Play pleasant music, even subliminal tapes of music geared to this buyer type with a marketing message blended into the program.

3. *Beware of the two-way value judgment.*

   Can you identify with this agent? It's a rainy Sunday afternoon. She's conducting an open house at her model from 1:00 PM until 5:00 PM. It's 4:50 PM and no one has been to the model. All of a sudden, a VW Bug pulls into the drive. A couple dressed in torn jeans, sweatshirts, sailing slickers and tattered tennis shoes hop out. The agent is sure they were looking for the new apartments a couple of miles away. "Why," the agent ponders, "am I always the one on duty when these kids show up! I'm trying to sell $200,000 and up single family homes!"

Wait a minute . . . These kids are looking at the agent through the front glass door and what they see is a very well-heeled professional who could double as a jewelry store mannequin. Quietly, the husband encourages his young wife not to ask questions, just to look. If they like the house, they'll talk to their banker at lunchtime on Monday.

This relationship is at a complete standstill before it gets started. Both parties have set up a value judgment. The agent has decided: "you're not qualified to buy," while the prospects have decided: "you're not sensitive to our needs and won't understand our financial position."

As a sales agent, you can only control your side of the judgment equation. This begins by greeting every consumer on an unbiased level. The young couple mentioned above, driving their sentimental old VW from college days, were relaxing on the weekend in old clothes. They're actually professionals with M.B.A. degrees and a bank account comfortable enough to purchase any home up to $250,000. In sales, you lose income when you judge your prospects by their cover!

4. *Establish trust*—ask questions which can be answered "yes," like:

"It's quite a day, isn't it?" "I see you found our model, didn't you?" "You'd like to see our homes, wouldn't you?"

5. *Use the power of a smile and a handshake.*

Stand up to greet your prospects. The power of a smile and a handshake can be visibly measured in the prospects who stay with you. Your handshake needs to be firm and accompanied by eye contact to be construed as genuine. There are three universal tools in this trade:

- Your smile
- Your appearance
- Your real estate knowledge

The Power Delivery of Your Card and Brochures

If your card and brochures are to have any value in the eyes of your consumers, you must create an interest in them through personalization and the timing of their presentation.

1. *How and when do you present the following?*

   ■ Your Card—Treasure your card and present it after you've gotten to know your prospect. Write a note on the back to encourage the prospect to keep it— make it a note that's special for the consumer.

   ■ Brochure—These are to be presented at the end of the showing of your homes. Preview the brochure with the prospect and note on the floor plans of their favorite homes the sales price "as of today's date." Create a little urgency. You may want to note special incentives or square footage.

2. *What do you give?*

   ■ Lookers get a card and a simple handout that gives a brief overview of your community.

   ■ Qualified buyers receive a primary brochure that visually, graphically and verbally captures the essence of your neighborhood. Again, personalize the brochure with specific information requested by the prospects. Make it "keepable" by making it noteworthy. Discard price, optional features price sheets and square footage pre-printed sheets. Hand-write this pertinent information on the floor plan the prospects loved. In this way, you'll be giving the prospects the most up-to-date information available—as well as a reason for them to call you back for additional figures. Price lists tend to become dated quickly and can confuse your buyers.

The Two Universal Communicator Styles: Open-End and Closed-End

When is the last time you greeted a prospect with a friendly handshake, warm smile and genuine comment such as, "It's a pleasure to have you in our homes today. How may I help you?" In response, the buyer spent 20 minutes telling you about his recent transfer to the area, his current residency at a local hotel—now into its fifth week—and the challenge he and his wife are having trying to manage three children under the age of six years in cramped quarters. He needs your help—right now—in solving his housing needs. He's our classic open-end communicator—the one who answers in great detail at every given opportunity. This communicator makes selling easier since you can track interest and motivation through verbosity. The open-end communicator needs questions to begin with—who, what, when, where and why—to create and encourage conversation. This communicator loves to talk!

The Closed-End Communicator

On the other hand, you can probably recall a time when you greeted another prospect with the simple greeting cited above, and the answer was short and simple: "Just want to see your houses." You might have responded with, "Are you looking for anything in particular?" The prospect answered, "Nope." You might have followed up with, "Is there a particular time limit you're working against?" The response of course was "not really."

What did you learn from your questions. Not one thing. Oh yes you did! You learned that you have a closed-end communicator. He doesn't want to talk and tries to answer everything in one or two words. This communicator makes your job more challenging. Now you *have* to give him all of the information you need within the questions so that all he does is confirm, deny, choose or correct the data...still a one or two word process!!

Going back to the previous questions, once you're certain a person is a closed-end communicator, it's better to say, "We offer single family homes and condominiums in Kiln Creek. Which would be of interest to you?" All he has to do is give you his choice. Then move into urgency. Ask "Do you need to purchase a new home within 30 days, 60 days or at no specific deadline?" Again, just a simple one or two word answer will do. Price can be determined through this same method of closed-end communication. Begin by asking, "Will your purchase be a cash transaction?" A yes or no answer will do. Then narrow the price gap by asking, "What price range do you desire?"

By communicating with your prospects in their communication comfort zone, you can enhance your rapport and become their confidant. Many consumers believe that salespeople are talkative and pushy—always striving to make those commission dollars. When you work to communicate with the buyer in a communication style comfortable to them, you're perceived as sensitive and insightful—a far cry from talkative and pushy.

You've heard and read repeatedly in sales training that the only thing you have to sell is yourself. That begins by developing and maintaining a solid base of rapport with everyone you greet.

Step 2: Qualifying and Counseling Prospects

When is the last time you looked forward to going to the doctor? You probably can answer "never!" Well, why not? Maybe it's because you get asked personal questions about diet, exercise or one of a hundred other topics. You also know that some of your answers may not be popular with the doctor while others would be viewed with a skeptical response. Perhaps you don't like doctor visits because you fear the unknown, or maybe you're afraid you'll be hurt.

Many of today's home buyers suffer a similar malady—REALTOR® reluctance. Although they are better informed as a result of media and public real estate seminars and may be veterans of home buying and selling, today's buyers remain apprehensive. They may fear the unknown, uncertain of your particular qualifying questions or procedures. A computer analysis, for example, that reduces the qualifying meeting to a statistical reflection of ratios, may be perfect for the well-qualified consumer and disastrous for the financially stretched consumer. The qualifying process can be a rigorous experience for even the most financially sound individual who simply is uncomfortable when having to answer personal questions asked by a relative stranger. Interestingly enough, the process is usually more difficult if you know the consumer well.

A Comfortable Qualifying Process

What do you do to make the process comfortable for all? The consistent application of a few simple courtesies should assure comfort for the majority of your purchasers.

Make the customers comfortable with you and the qualifying environment by taking a sincere interest in their problem, listening attentively with steady eye contact and having no interruptions while they explain their home buying needs. Use your phone answering machine when talking with a purchaser onsite, so that you will not be interrupted. Conduct the interview in a confidential environment behind closed doors. Preferably, this area is set up as a casual conversation area with low lighting, attractive art work and no phone, desk or other sales tools that imply "high pressure sales." Offer the prospects a beverage while you talk.

Begin the interview by explaining why you qualify. An effective way to break the ice is simply to say, "Before we discuss several questions, I'd like to ask if you are planning to pay cash for your new home?" Typically, the response is an exchange of smiles, laughter and a comfortable feeling of being flattered that for one moment in time, you, the REALTOR®, felt that these consumers could be paying cash. If you're lucky and the answer is "yes," the financial qualifying interview moves quickly to a brief discussion of confirming the sources of the cash available to purchase their home.

If the answer is "no," and a loan will be used to finance the sale, take a few minutes to explain the role of the lender in the home buying process and help the consumer understand that the questions you need to ask about employment and finances are the same ones that will be asked by the lender. Explain further that the reason for the questions is a desire to determine the maximum amount the lender will lend.

Ask your customers if they have any questions they'd like to ask about the qualifying interview before you begin the questions. Then, outline the three areas you'll be discussing so they know what to expect. Financial qualifying will discuss:

- Current income

- Fixed commitments

- Assets (always save this for last to end on a positive note)

- Practical features the prospects want in a home (practical needs)

- Emotional needs (features the prospects love about their prospective new home and that they definitely want)

To maintain customer comfort while you move through the financial qualification process, begin by asking *each* purchaser to tell you about their employment. A simple approach is to ask:

- "Where are you employed?"

- "What is your position in the company?" (This shows a personal interest in them.)

- "How long have you been with the company?" If the answer is less than three years, ask what they did before going to work for that company.

- "What is your annual compensation for your current position?" "Are there additional bonuses or commissions? Discuss them, please." Be sure to conclude this section of questioning by asking, "Do you currently have any additional sources of income?"

These could include second jobs, investment income, alimony or child support, so be certain you ask about these. Now you have the buyer's income record.

■ Discuss fixed commitments openly and empathetically. Explain that a fixed commitment is one that will not be paid off in full by equal monthly installments within the prescribed limit of the lender and mortgage you plan to use. These limits vary from six to nine months.

Shop for these commitments by mentioning auto payments, bank loans, finance company loans, furniture payments, education loans, credit cards and medical or dental commitments. Carefully monitor your nonverbal responses to the answers.

If the purchasers answer that they have no debts and you jump up and down for joy, they may sense that you're only focused on a future commission. (It really is important to stay objective and empathetic.)

This is also an appropriate time to ask about previous credit problems. Listen and do not pass judgment. Let the prospects explain in full any previous problems and then discuss candidly what must be done to correct the problem. Offer your counsel and direction in the process and help your prospects understand that they're not the only home buyers who've had to deal with problem credit.

If the news is so negative that you know for certain they must regroup, pay off old debt and build a current payment history before qualifying for a mortgage, counsel them in that direction. They will value your candor and probably embrace your professional information as their plan of action for rebuilding their financial future.

Questions for Qualifying Practical Needs

At this point, review the five kinds of qualifying questions we use and note what each question tells us.

The Five Kinds of Qualifying Questions:

1. *Urgency*—"How soon will you be needing a new home?"

2. *Ability to Pay*—"Where do you work?" or "Our prices range from $____ to $____. Is that what you had in mind?"

3. *Practical Needs*—"Who is the home for?" or "We offer three and four bedroom homes here. Is that what you had in mind?"

4. *Emotional Wants or Needs*—"Our homeowners' association includes a pool. Is that something you would use?"

5. *Decision-Making Authority*—"Is there anyone else who will be involved in making this decision?"

Practical needs represent all of the fundamental features that the home must have including number of bedrooms and baths, room arrangement, location, price, terms of the sale and any specific feature such as a shop area in the garage or bonus room in the attic for a playroom. The practical needs are the no frills needs of the family. The following questions may help you identify practical needs. Jot them on an index card that you keep in your briefcase or work notebook for immediate reference. Add your favorites to this list.

- "Tell me your bedroom, bath and room arrangement requirements."
- "Tell me what you can't live without in your next home."
- "Where are you living now?" "Are you renting or purchasing?" "Must you sell before you buy?"
- "Describe the kitchen you need."
- "Describe the outdoor features your home must have."
- "What's the maximum commute you can tolerate?"
- "What price range is comfortable for you?"
- "What initial investment do you plan to make?"
- "What monthly payment will work well with your budget?"
- "Are you limited to a specific school district, side of town or recreational area?" (Sometimes the buyer insists on close proximity to tennis courts, pools, lakes, parks, etc.)

The Emotional Needs Analysis

Have you ever gone shopping to buy a new suit with an absolute image of what you want including color, fabric, finish features and design, only to return home hours later with a sport coat and slacks or skirt that weren't the color, fabric, style or finish you had wanted just a few hours earlier? Home buying is very similar to suit buying. When buying a suit, you know you need clothing. When buying a home, you know you need shelter. In both cases, you have fundamental requirements to be met such as size and price, but beyond that, you are greatly influenced by your emotional needs.

Our real estate industry has reported consistently and repeatedly that every home buyer's decision involves two sets of needs: practical (which comprise 20 percent of the buying decision) and emotional (which comprise 80 percent of the decision).

That emphatically illustrates the need to know your customers' emotional needs and how important it is for you to find a property that satisfies the majority of those needs—within the buyer's financial parameters.

Again, transfer these questions to an index card and enjoy using them with your customers.

Emotional Needs Questions:

1. What did you absolutely love in your previous homes? (This can be modified to say apartment or condominium for first-time purchasers.) This answer tells you what your customers won't live without.

2. What did you completely dislike about your last home? (This tells you what to avoid.)

3. What comfort features are a must for you?

   - Fireplace
   - Jacuzzi
   - Security System
   - Intercom
   - Control Stereo System
   - Gourmet Kitchen
   - Luxurious Master Bath
   - Private Master Suite
   - Fenced Yard for Children or Pets
   - Dramatic Ceilings, Windows, Built-ins
   - An Enormous Lawn with Exquisite Landscaping

This answer tells you what will influence 80 percent of your customers' decision—so listen carefully. Also, be aware of what they *don't* say—what you can perceive from their general ambiance, social circle or professional requirements. Remember, *80 percent* of their buying decision will be based on their emotional needs!

Information Giving

In the qualifying process, you must use a sense of fairness and balance with your customer. Rather than end the session with a battery of questions, spend a while reviewing basic information that every customer would appreciate.

Review with them the list of services that you provide for every new home purchaser. Such a list is shown in Exhibit 4.1 on page 48. Give this "New Home REALTOR® Services to Buyer" sheet to your prospects.

Area Discussion

Introduce your prospect to the area in which your community is located. An area map (see Exhibit 4.2 on page 50) is very helpful in this introduction. Be sure to point out schools, recreation, shopping, cultural and employment centers. Review the following:

- Area sets the price.

- Ask: "Are you familiar with this area of town?"

- "What would you like to know about this area?"

Builder Introduction

To make your builder a real person to the purchasers, show photos of the builder and list the builder's professional credentials, a list of previous communities he or she has built and awards and recognition he or she has received. Be sure to ask your prospects if they've ever lived in one of this builder's homes before. Quote satisfied customers who praise the builder's work. Nothing is better at this point than giving the prospective purchaser several letters of endorsement from satisfied customers. It is even more effective to provide your prospect with the phone numbers of those customers (with their permission, of course) so they can talk with them directly. Do include a builder storyboard in your models or sales center as a third party silent endorsement to all you've been saying about the builder.

Community Profile

Remember the doctor's visit story that started this chapter? Be reminded that it's your job as a sales professional to remove the fear of the

Exhibit 4.1 **New Home REALTOR® Services to Buyer**

- Interview to determine buyer needs—both practical and emotional.

- Determine loan amount available based on financial qualification.

- Preview the community and all site amenities.

- Preview furnished model homes and:

  - review renderings of all homes;

  - review floor plans and provide copies; and

  - review site plan and point out schools, shopping and employment.

- Construct a contract to reflect buyer financial preferences.

- Assist with interior selections.

- Assist with loan application beginning with the scheduling of the application. Pre-sell customers to the lender before you send them to the bank. Attend the loan application with the purchaser if they desire your presence.

- Follow up weekly with loan and building status and then update the purchaser.

- Notify purchasers of additional loan exhibits needed **as requested** by lender.

- Notify purchasers of home completion date.

- Schedule walk-thru inspection with the builder representative, the buyer and you. Prepare a walk-thru inspection sheet.

- Schedule closing with attorney.

- Notify purchasers of the exact amount of certified funds necessary to close.

- Attend the closing with purchasers to further review closing figures and documents and to give the keys, punch list form and home warranties to the buyer.

- Stay in touch after the sale to pick up the 30-day punch list requests and to follow through with the builder to see that these items are completed in a timely manner.

- Host a housewarming party with the new buyers within 30 to 90 days of purchase.

unknown. Put your prospective purchasers at ease by previewing your community while you're still in your sales center or model home. Preview the following:

- The site map that visually shows them the master plan (refer to Exhibit 4.3 on page 51)

- Community amenities, such as recreational features and common green areas, cul-de-sacs for traffic control, special lighting throughout the neighborhood and aesthetic features, including small parks, ponds, jogging or walking trails, bird watching and private picnicking areas

- Community facts, including acreage, total number of homes to be built, types of homes, price ranges, sources of water, types of sewage systems, neighborhood security systems and homeowner's association

Remember, AREA—BUILDER—COMMUNITY information and qualifying happen in the sales center before demonstration of the models.

Knock-Out Questions for High-Traffic Days

What do you do when you're at the model or sales center and several prospects arrive simultaneously or in close proximity to one another? It's simple. You have to define the most likely purchaser from the group. Use *knockout questions* that separate the lookers from the immediate purchasers. Greet each prospect warmly with a handshake and a smile, exchange introductions and then ask one or two of these knock-out questions:

- "How long have you been looking for a new home?"

- "Do you have a home to sell before you buy?" If the answer is "yes," ask: "Is it listed?" "For how long?" "Is it sold?" "When does it close?"

- "Are all of the decision makers involved in making your purchase with you today?"

- "If you find a home that meets all of your practical and emotional needs, are you in a position to authorize a contract today?"

- "Did you bring your checkbook with you?"

As you can see, the questions are designed to weed out the most qualified, urgent purchaser. Be forewarned, however, even if prospects knock themselves out as primary prospects for the moment, do ask how you might help them. Invite them to browse through your exhibits in the sales center, to view a community video or to simply enjoy a beverage break

Exhibit 4.2   Area Map

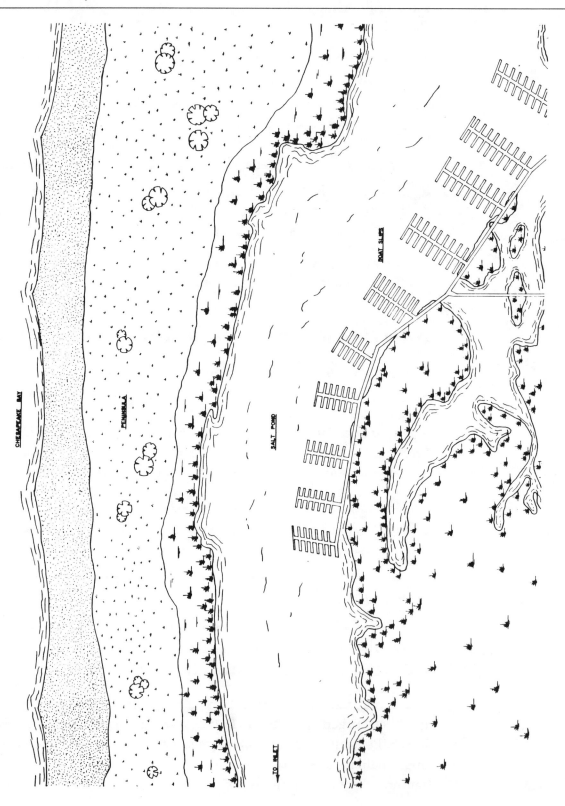

Exhibit 4.3   Site Map

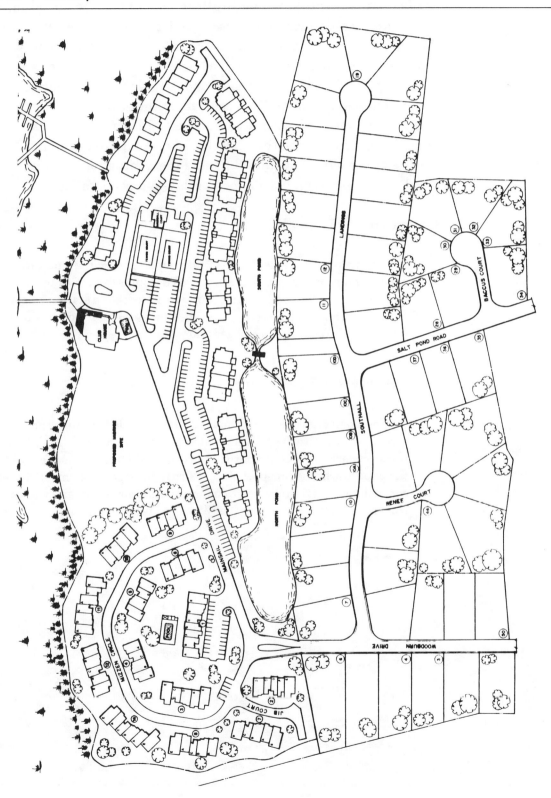

(which you provide) until you can get back to meet with them. If you're really tied up, offer to schedule an alternate time to show them your homes or call in a back-up agent or hostess to assist them. The one alternative you don't want is to have the prospects wander through the models without a professional sales presentation. The homes only have one opportunity to make a powerful first impression and you want to be there to capture buying interest and motivate a contract authorization.

Enjoy solving the following case studies, thinking about how you would apply the information in this chapter. To make it even more fun, ask your friends at the office how they'd handle these situations and transfer the problem-solving techniques into your day-to-day operation.

Case Study #1: Qualifying

The agent has greeted and is finishing up preliminary qualifying in the sales center. Prospects are an engaged couple and so far fit 'A' buyer qualifications. The agent turns around to notice that a station wagon pulling a U-Haul trailer has parked. Three kids and a couple start toward the door to the office. What does the agent do?

Case Study #2: Qualifying

The agent has taken an 'A' buyer on a second visit through the models and has shown the prospect an available home in inventory. Agent closes the prospect back in the confidential area of the sales center. As the agent begins the paperwork, the prospect states, 'I really need to have my dad check this construction out first. He's very handy at building things and will be visiting from Montana in three months.' What does the agent do?

5

The Third and Fourth Essential Steps To Selling New Homes: Demonstration and Financing

This chapter takes you through steps three and four of the *Five Essential Steps of New Home Selling*: demonstrating the product and presenting financing alternatives. Demonstrating the product requires skill and thorough product knowledge. Included in this chapter are charts, floor plans, an explanation of the critical path to sales and simple steps to implement in your product demonstration that involve your purchasers and put you in control of the sales process.

While demonstrating your product, you will also be practicing the salesperson's claim to fame, overcoming objections. The better you are at overcoming objections, the more sales you will make, the more awards you will receive and the more willing you will be to overcome future objections.

During the discussion of demonstration, there are repeated references to closing. Closing the sale is the final step of the Five Essential Steps and will be addressed in the next chapter. In sales, however, it must be acknowledged that closing is a procedure to follow from the start to the finish of every transaction; nowhere is this truer than in the demonstration of the product. You are guiding a "yes" momentum to carry the sale. As you overcome objections, do not be afraid to "ask for the order."

You may sell the prospect on your product, but in most cases it will take financing to make the dream come true for both of you. The salesperson who is an expert on financing alternatives will close more sales. The subject of financing is a bewildering one, particularly for first-time buyers. The second part of this chapter gives you guidelines for the type of information you should always have available. Provide this information at various times during the sales process. If a prospect asks a financing question during the demonstration, that is a strong buying signal. You may close then and present financing information while you draw up the contract.

Step 3: Demonstrating the Product and the Community

Following is a list of tips that make new home sales very different from the resale business.

- The sale involves using the FEATURE-BENEFIT-INVOLVEMENT Technique (reviewed in detail on pages 58 and 64-66).

- Architectural advantages make for easy living.

- There are more energy-saving features.

- You must *demonstrate* rather than letting your prospects discover.

- You can paint a picture of the neighborhood's future.

- There are no offer-counteroffer hassles. Builders strive to sell at a specific price.

- You must be able to skillfully qualify the buyers.

- There is no one to move out.

- Buying a new home strokes the ego.

New homes offer the most innovative features and systems available in the industry. Many prospects who visit your site are not familiar with the newest security systems, appliances or comfort features. As a result there is an opportunity for confusion and possible rejection. To avoid this, simplify operation of the systems and features through demonstration.

Professional Language

In the process, it's extremely important to use language that appeals to the consumer and makes it easy for them to accept. Take the following Self-Test and see how you score. Be creative in your answers. Use alternative words or phrases to define the following:

Self-Test

1. Condo _____

2. Deposit _____

3. Lot _____

4. Project/Job _____

5. Afford _____

6. Deal _____

7. Sell _____

8. Execute _____

9. Entry _____

10. Family Room _____

11. Living Room/Dining Room _____

12. Kitchen _____

13. Master Bedroom _____

14. Upstairs Bedroom _____

15. Large Closet _____

16. Upgraded Bathtub _____

17. Dishwasher _____

18. Standard Features _____

19. Upgrades _____

20. Price _____

Now for the answers:

1. _____ home with condominium ownership.

   Fill in the blank that's appropriate for your community—affordable, conveniently located, prestigious, private, waterfront, etc.

2. Initial investment

3. Home site

4. Neighborhood or community

5. What payment will be *comfortable* for you?

6. Opportunity

7. Help you buy

8. Authorize

9. Greeting area/foyer

10. Gathering room/casual living area

11. Formal areas

12. Indoor eating area/food galley

13. Owner's suite

14. Children's suite/guest area

15. Wardrobe area

16. Luxury bath

17. Use the name brand of every appliance.

18. Custom benefits that come with your home

19. Personal pluses

20. Premium

The Critical Path to Sales

Like every objective you strive to attain in sales, you must first develop a plan of action to accomplish it. When showing a home, your objective is to sell the property. With that in mind, you must develop a specific plan of what properties to show, in what order and—once at the property—what should be shown first, second, third through closing. This process is defined as *Developing the Critical Path to Sales*. The path varies depending upon the customer. Your qualifying interview clearly helps you determine what properties meet both the practical and emotional needs of the prospect. Experience has proven that you never show the dream house first. Why not? Because most people want to feel they've really made a home buying decision cautiously. They will seldom make a decision without having seen several homes to use as a basis of comparison.

Study the following list, which summarizes the critical path to sales.

1. Welcome the "guests" in the foyer. Prospects should never enter through a back door, even if you must go to a side or rear lockbox to obtain keys.

2. Move prospects to your model home or sales center information area.

    ■ Make it your goal to (BRIEFLY!) familiarize the guests with all of the boards and visuals of the community. (Remember they have to see the community to fall in love.)

3. Tour the site with the guests pointing out:

    ■ amenities, including clubhouse;

    ■ available lots;

    ■ green common areas (which give the illusion of added space);

    ■ several different homes that demonstrate available floor plans. Guests must be taken through these homes so they can touch and feel. Be certain the tour ends in the room that has the most emotional appeal for this buyer.

4. Guide the guests to the refreshment area. Offer them a beverage. While in this area, select the generic brochure and any other material you feel is appropriate to take to the *CLOSING ROOM*. Always take a contract and a calculator.

5. Ask the guests to complete a registration card while you're getting a brochure for them.

    ■ "Would you like a brochure about our community? Great! Please fill in our guest card while I get you one. We would appreciate any comments you have about our neighborhood, our amenities and particularly any of our homes."

6. Move to the *CLOSING ROOM*. Remember the purpose of this move is:

    ■ to answer questions, and

    ■ to reconfirm/requalify the buyer's emotional and practical needs.

As you review the property that best meets these needs, your objective is to *ASK FOR THE ORDER*. This may be the first of several visits for these buyers but you want to condition them by asking for the order each time. You may find that you ask for the order and initiate writing the contract while still in their favorite room of the model home of their choice. That's an excellent way to maintain an emotional high while keeping your buyers very comfortable.

During your demonstration, remember that you are selling the community as well as the home.

1. Use the community theme often during your presentation.

2. Be able to adjust your presentation to different prospects—speed up, slow down, focus on different parts for different people.

3. Know two or three key words for each lifestyle home in order to appeal to the targeted buyer for that home type.

Rate yourself to evaluate how you have done after each presentation including the areas of the greeting, qualifying, financial, practical and emotional needs and demonstrating the property.

Plotting Your Critical Path

It's time to dress up and play ball. Exhibit 5.1 shows floor plans of luxury condominiums. Imagine showing the homes to the following two families. Remember that the critical path must be customized for the individual purchaser and should end in the room that has the greatest appeal for this buyer type. Use different colored pens and plot your critical paths.

Family of Four: Mom, dad, two children, 8 and 10 years of age. Both parents are employed full-time.

Alternative Family: A middle-age couple who are "DINKS"—double-income, no kids. The husband would like to enjoy his woodworking hobby in a garage shop.

Exhibit 5.2 on pages 62 and 63 shows the floor plan of a sales center. The drawing is run twice. On the first floor plan, plot your path to guide a prospect through the sales center. The author's suggested critical path appears on the second drawing.

F.B.I. Approach—Feature, Benefit, Involvement

Once you have developed your critical path of showing and committed yourself to demonstrating the product, you may find it extremely beneficial to involve your customers in the showing using the Feature—Benefit—Involvement technique. Simply defined, this technique has you pointing out to the home buyer a particular feature of the home such as the brick exterior. Next you talk about its benefits—in the case of brick, no maintenance. Finally, you involve the customers by asking them a question such as "Are you looking for a home that requires little or no exterior maintenance?" The more you involve the prospect, the higher the likelihood that you will close them for the order. Remember to use the F.B.I. approach to sell homes:

- *Features*—State exactly what they are.

- *Benefit*—Sell the benefits of the feature to the buyer.

- *Involvement*—Use a partial close—physical involvement "Feel this"—or a question to qualify them.

Exhibit 5.1   **Townhouse Floor Plan**

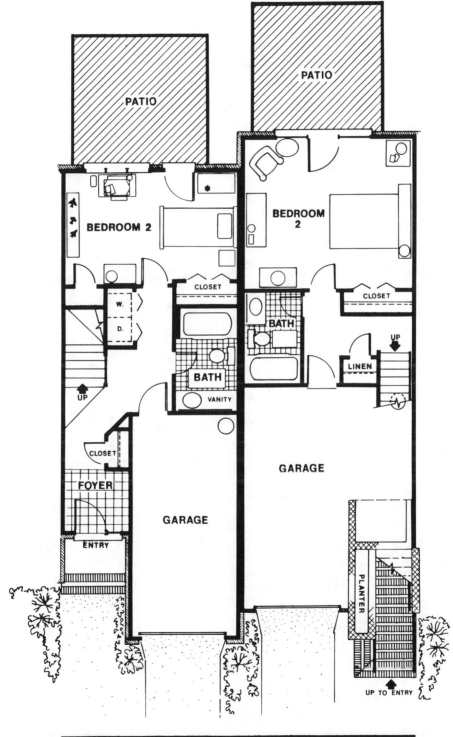

FIRST FLOOR

Exhibit 5.1 (cont'd) Townhouse Floor Plan

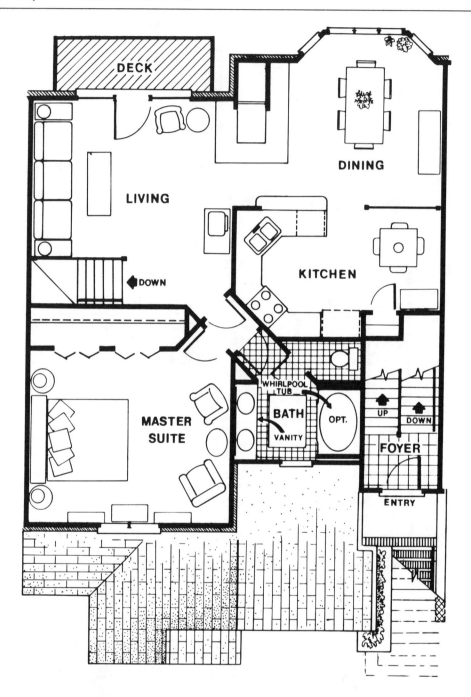

SECOND FLOOR

Exhibit 5.1 (cont'd)   Townhouse Floor Plan

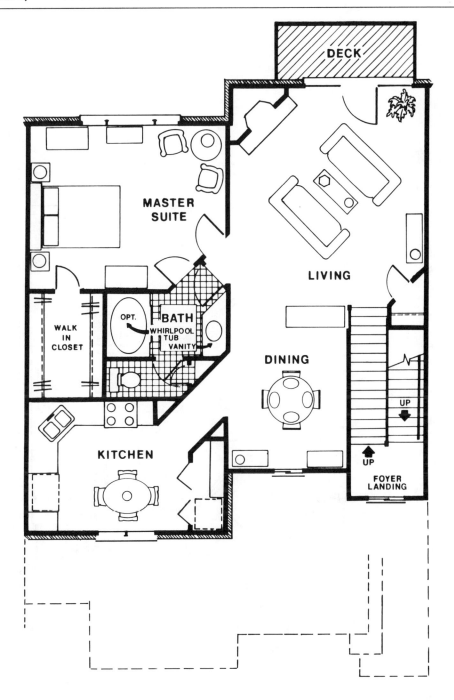

THIRD FLOOR

Exhibit 5.2   Townhouse Floor Plan

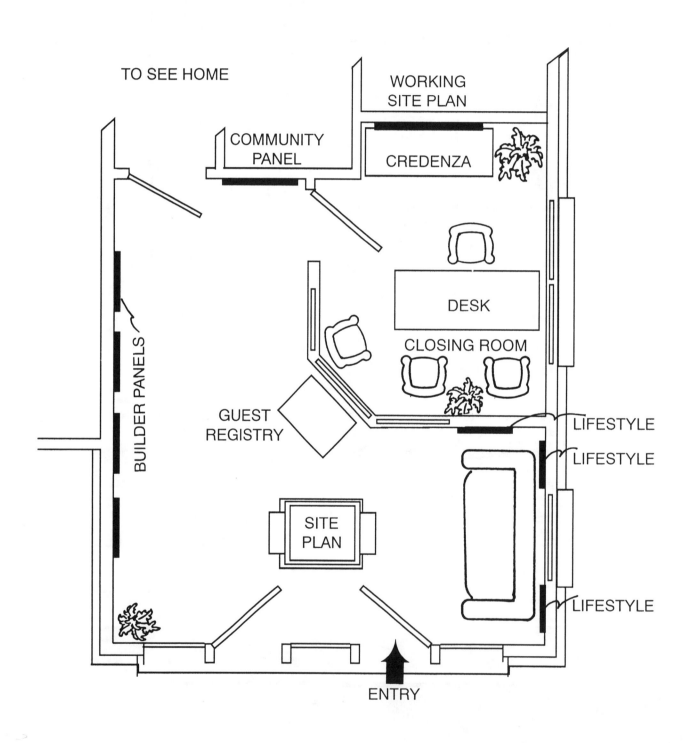

Exhibit 5.2 (cont'd) **Townhouse Floor Plan**

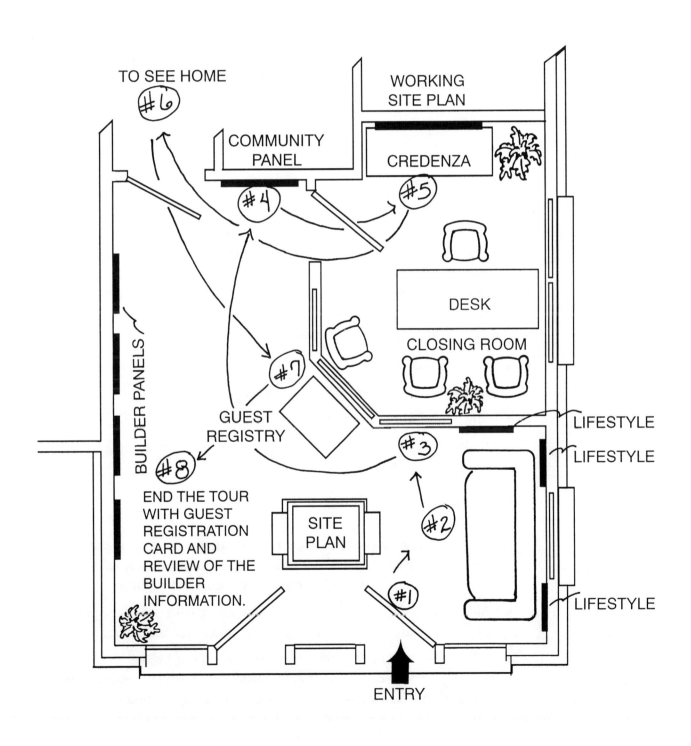

Consider the following example from the perspective of the Feature-Benefit-Involvement technique. As you are showing the property, the prospects begin feeling the wallpaper in the kitchen, talking to each other and taking great interest in your demonstration of the microwave oven. Close then by saying "This kitchen is not only beautifully wallpapered, its appliances are convenient and easy to operate. Wouldn't you agree?"

If they object to the size of the oven or some other kitchen feature, acknowledge the objection by repeating it back, identify the specific problem and isolate the fact that if the builder offered a large oven in this home, they'd be ready to buy the home. If they start listing other objections, it may be time to move to another home. If not, you've got a sale. So, ask for that order.

Involve the Prospect

As you prepare to show property to your buying prospects, remember your first day on a sports team, dance troupe or as a cheerleader. While the coach or teacher told you what you could expect, you really wanted to be shown what to do, how to do it and you wanted to be *involved*—listening—asking questions—getting answers and *doing* the assigned task. Home buyers are no different. They want you to demonstrate and they want to be involved. The following tips make showing and demonstrating the property much more effective. Your demonstration should:

- offer an opportunity for critical evaluation of the product;

- make the buyer feel comfortable with the product;

- allow time to point out hidden values;

- make you look like a "sensitive salesperson" by removing fear factors.

Use Features and Benefits To Sell Value

- State brand names when showing appliances, heating and air conditioning systems, carpets, bath fixtures, windows, doors, shingles and any other component with a name associated with quality.

- Make the model come alive and become a home by having the prospects place furniture and describe how they would use particular spaces.

- "One of the special features we offer in all of our homes is ___. Is that something you can use?" (This could be upgraded carpet, special appliances, security systems, and/or special warranties.)

- "Five things that this builder offers here that you won't find anywhere else in this price range are:" (*BUILD INTEREST*.)

- Standard features—make sure to point out all the builder choices that come with the home at no extra charge/included in the costs/free.

- Point out decorator/optional features.

- "We've had an interior design firm decorate to show how this home can be personalized and how space might best be utilized. Is that important and something you'd like in your home? How would you use this area?"

- Options can add to the cost: "That (bookcase/upgraded carpet/etc.) is beautiful. It's an additional cost, and in a few minutes when we have a chance to sit down and talk, I'll show you how it would fit into your mortgage payment."

- Use a checklist to point out everything in the models.

- Shop your competition—your prospects may offer some comparisons.

- Lights-Action-Sell. Turn on all the lights (shadows make rooms look smaller.) Keep your performance like grand opening day—every day.

- Show the most dramatic feature/room last. This will vary from prospect to prospect. For example: To a large family, emphasize the family room; to senior citizens, the formal areas for entertaining; and to young marrieds, the master suite.

- Time yourself and try to keep the prospects involved with your property and not looking at the competition.

- Tell—don't ask—the prospects to become involved.

- Demonstrate a one-of-a-kind home they can buy TODAY.

- Take prospects to a product/inventory home of the model/type they have chosen (a maximum of two or three).

- Decide in advance which homes or models you want/need to sell.

- Stay with the prospect until YOU decide they are not qualified.

- Keep a record of the number of prospects taken to a one-of-a-kind home.

While You're Demonstrating . . .

- Introduce your graphic exhibits and know the material on each graphic.

- Add more information than what the prospects can read themselves.

- Ask further qualifying questions as you follow the CRITICAL PATH.

- Personalize your presentation. Keep trying to make a friend feel comfortable, to rely on you and ask you questions.

- Talk up the video presentation. Use enthusiastic, interest-building language so the prospects stay to watch it.

A Final Thought

As you perfect your demonstration skills, remember that each prospective buyer of any major purchase must become emotionally involved with the product whether it's:

- trying on a mink coat before buying it;

- driving a new car before taking it home to stay;

- or . . . learning to operate the features of a new home before buying.

It's up to you to create a warm environment within your homes to allow the prospects to become students as they explore new designs, new features and new systems that will make every day Christmas in their new home. Make your classroom (model) the best in your marketplace—not only in quality, design and merchandising, but most importantly in the area of professional sensitivity—by teaching your prospects the fascinating benefits of your homes. Your expertise in product demonstration will determine to a great extent the number of A+ buyers you'll enjoy.

Step 4:   Knowing the Financing Alternatives

Sales success in New Homes is directly related to your financial expertise in the mortgage marketplace. You must maintain up-to-date information about every type of mortgage within your marketplace if you are to *successfully* negotiate a wide range of sales with a varied spectrum of purchases. It's been accurately reported that: "Some of us in sales have had one sale a hundred times over. Others of us have had 100 sales that were each customized in their mortgage needs."

Agents in new home sales typically offer a basic package of loans to their customers, usually a VA or FHA loan, a conventional mortgage with fixed rate and, if they're just a little creative, an adjustable rate conventional mortgage. The result of this limited package of loans is the probability of missed sales to nonconforming borrowers in today's marketplace.

If your goal is to develop consistent perfection in sales, you constantly need to expand your knowledge of mortgage instruments and any changes taking place in mortgage underwriting standards. Such changes affect your ability to qualify purchases on a daily basis. Read the mortgage update bulletins published daily by area mortgage centers and meet regularly with a mortgage lender for briefings of anticipated and actual changes in the mortgage market. If your firm is computer-linked to primary lenders in your marketplace, you can check daily for updates and changes.

Why not simply call your lender to qualify your purchasers? What happens when:

- you need to know what price range home to show prospects and your lender is not available to prequalify them? Where is your credibility if you cannot sit down and qualify them? Where is your professionalism if you show prospects properties for which they will not qualify?

- the purchasers come to you and ask you to discuss the advantages and disadvantages of two loans that they have been independently comparing, and you don't have a clue as to how to respond? But wait—your lender can help you out. You guessed it! The lender is unavailable. What's next?

A primary component to your sales success involves your skill and thorough knowledge of a wide range of loan instruments for both conforming and nonconforming clients. Conforming borrowers are those who meet the underwriting guidelines of "Fannie Mae" (the Federal National Mortgage Association operated by the government as a secondary market for federally insured loans) and "Freddie Mac" (the Federal Home Loan Mortgage Corporation, a government agency that guarantees mortgages for savings and loan associations only). Another corporation that requires buyer conformity to specific underwriting guidelines is "Ginnie Mae" (the Government National Mortgage Association, a corporation that buys and sells mortgages from lenders to keep long-term investment money moving).

Nonconforming purchasers are those whose financial background will not conform to the three sets of agency standards required through Ginnie Mae, Fannie Mae and Freddie Mac. Such purchasers may be self-employed individuals with less that three years of self-employed history or first time purchasers with less than three years on a job with no credit references (for example, if their auto was a gift and all of their purchases have been cash). You often must locate funding sources for nonconforming borrowers and typically that begins with local, hometown savings and loans or banks who warehouse their loans in-house. Since they don't sell their loans to be the secondary marketplace, the customers of such banks do not have to conform to the qualifying demands of conforming loan institutions. Nonconforming lenders typically evaluate and approve loans on a case by case approach.

This section of the book is designed, not to teach you finance, but to provide you with primary resources that can be located in every marketplace in America.

Common Mortgage Types

The four common mortgage types available today are:

- Veteran Administration loans, referred to as VA loans, which have low initial investment requirements depending upon the veteran's term of service as well as previous VA loan commitments still outstanding. These loans are available through local mortgage lenders and savings and loans.

- FHA loans are available to purchasers with lower initial investment (down payment) requirements that reduce the amount of cash needed at the time of the purchase. Numerous types of FHA loans are available today through banks and savings and loans.

- Conventional financing for conforming customers typically is available through local savings and loans as well as banks. Traditionally, these loans require a higher initial investment (down payment).

- Nonconforming conventional loans are available to purchasers who do not meet the underwriting standards of the secondary mortgage market. These loans are available through private investors, insurance company investment divisions and hometown lenders who no not resell their loans to the secondary markets. Nonconforming lenders exercise flexibility in initial investment requirements, debt-to-income ratios and terms of prepayment.

Mortgage Information

The best resource for loan information is your local lender—a savings and loan institution or the mortgage division of an area bank. It is important to develop rapport with area lenders who offer each of the primary types of loans. Schedule an appointment to meet with the local lenders you've selected to supply the loans necessary for your customers.

Interview the lenders, acknowledging that you are shopping for mortgage packages for your clients. Help them understand that they must be *competitive* to be attractive. Ask questions that deal with the following:

- Types of mortgages they offer.

- Underwriting requirements for each including:

  1. The maximum allowed housing ratio-housing debt as a portion of gross income

  2. The maximum allowed total debt ratio—total long-term debt including housing, as a portion of gross income

  3. Points charged for the loan (Find out norm against current market trends. Are they equal to, higher than or below market trends?)

  4. Loan Origination Fees charged (Ask if these are reduced as you bring a certain volume of business to this lender.)

  5. An itemized schedule of closing costs including fees other than points that may be charged

  6. The period of time your loan can expect to be in their underwriting department (If you feel the period of time stated is longer than the competition, discuss this.)

  7. Whether underwriting is done locally (If not, ask for the specifics of who, where, when and again, how long underwriting will take.)

  8. The ratio of approved loans to loans submitted to underwriting (If there's a high fallout rate—beware!!)

  9. If the loans are funded *locally* for closing (If funds for closing are supplied from out-of-town offices, have the process explained in detail. Investigate, by talking to closing attorneys who have handled a lot of their loans, what kind of closing delays, if any, have resulted from long distance funding.)

  10. What is done to provide weekly status reports on each of the loans you might have in process (You are seeking a lender that has a system for regular, weekly reporting in writing.)

  11. The methods used by the lender to update you about new loans in the marketplace or changes in existing loans

  12. The lender's company history and successes (Your objective is to determine company stability, source of funding—are they selling loans into the secondary market—as well as their major mortgage loan officers.)

13.   What services they offer to the buyer and to you, the REALTOR®

14.   Their policy concerning loan default and/or prepayment penalties

15.   Their policy of loan assumption (Do they offer loan assumption mortgages and, if so, what fees are involved? What qualification criteria must the new borrower meet, if any?)

There is no replacement for building strong relationships with lenders who are available to supply a wide range of mortgages to a variety of purchasers. Keep them competitive and maintain constant lines of communication to retain an advantage in your marketplace.

The Realty Blue Book is a second vital resource for ready availability of fundamental loan information. Once you subscribe to this book's annual update services, you will regularly receive information that supplements and/or replaces existing textual information. The book contains descriptions as well as clauses and phrases to use in drafting your sales contracts. It is easy to keep in your briefcase and is second only to having a financial genie in your pocket. To order, call (800) 288-2006 or write to: Professional Publishing Corporation, 122 Paul Drive, San Rafael, CA 94903. Check to see if your local Board of REALTORS® sells this book to area members. Financial knowledge and skills require constant updating if you are to offer the most attractive loan services to your purchasers.

The Fifth Essential Step To Selling New Homes: Closing the Sale

Closing the sale is the final step of the Five Essential Steps to selling new homes. It is important to realize that closing is not an event that occurs once the demonstration is completed. Rather, it begins the moment you recognize that a prospect has an interest in your product. It is a *process* that requires professional sensitivity to the buying signs the prospect expresses along the way. This chapter is designed to introduce you to your role in the closing cycle, the buyer's response and how to interpret it, as well as specific strategies for closing the sale. Try the techniques you feel will enhance your success in the closing arena.

The Salesperson's Lead

Your professional sales training has taught you repeatedly that you are expected by the buyer to ASK FOR THE ORDER—in other words, close the sale. But if closing is expected, why are so many REALTORS® reluctant to ask for that order? Veteran sales agents will respond, "I'm not reluctant. I don't feel I've done my job if I haven't asked for the order. Certainly there will be no commission until I make a sale." Other agents experience tremendous anxiety and sheer fear when confronted with the closing process. Agents in that mode become museum keepers. Daily they open model homes in spit'n polish condition, conduct tours through the property and smile politely as the prospects leave, saying, "Call me when I can help you." In other words, let me know when you've sold yourself, and I'll write the contract!

Your lead in the closing cycle is a three-step process . . .

1. Listen carefully to the prospects' questions and observations about the property. The more specific the questions the better, since only an *interested* prospect wants specific information!

2. Observe carefully the prospects' nonverbal communication including:

    ■ Touching or feeling the property

    ■ Lingering in a specific area of the home

    ■ Exchanging glances/touches with a spouse (or other decision maker)

3. Ask for the order *throughout* the showing of the property to establish a "yes" momentum through a series of closing questions that result in a yes answer.

As you use these three steps, you must also prepare yourself for rejection. Appreciate the fact that "no" answers in real estate sales are necessary to get to the "yes" answers that lead to a sale. Real estate professionals are like Babe Ruth. In order to become the number one home run king in major league baseball, Ruth first had to become the strikeout king. He had no fear of failure because he understood that the only shot at hitting a home run involved picking up the bat and going to home plate to face the pitcher. You can only succeed in sales when you are willing to use your closing skills when you face prospective buyers. The choice is yours . . . bench warmer or major league.

The Buyer's Response: Raising Objections

It's important to encourage buyers to talk to you so you will be able to determine if they have any objections to the home you show them. They won't buy until their objections are addressed.

All You Ever Wanted To Know about Objections!

1. What is an objection?

    ■ A natural part of making a decision

- A process of evaluation

- A plea for support from the salesperson and other people

- A point for discussion

2. Use sales office tools to verify your answers to objections such as copies of:

   - Brochures

   - Plots

   - Homeowner association documents

   - Standard features outline (this can be in your own handwriting)

   - Warranty information

   - Financial details

3. Use the feel-felt-found method to overcome objections. "I can appreciate how you *feel*. One of our recent homeowners felt the same way (about the electricity bill, noise level, etc.) when he was looking here. What he found was that his actual power savings are substantial (show actual bill). He doesn't hear other homeowners' radios or TVs."

4. Question the objection to determine it's validity. "Is that important to you?" "How important is that to you?" "Would you like to see the manufacturer's brochure on the fireplace?" Once you determine the seriousness of the objection, you know you must overcome it, overlook it or go to another property.

5. When dealing with room size objections, discuss how the room will be used. If the area fits the usage, size becomes a non-problem.

6. Clarify the emotional reactions or objections by asking the buyer specific questions after showing a home:

   - "What do you like about the home?"

   - "How do you feel about the home?"

   - "What don't you like about the home?"

   - "How does this home compare with your 'dream home'?"

7. Let the prospects express their opinions. Ask general questions to get them talking.

8. Let them use you as a sounding board. Put them at ease so they will trust your ideas.

9. Ask probing questions.

- ■ "What do you like about the kitchen?"

- ■ "What don't you like about the family room?"

10. Use trial questions to determine if the home really interests them.

Overcoming Objections

Try implementing these steps to solve and sort objections. Remember, not all objections can be solved to the point of sale, but they can all be identified as solvable or insurmountable. These steps will help you in solving the solvable.

1. Agree with the prospects—it helps to diffuse their defense mechanism.

2. Feed back prospect objections! Let them hear what they are saying.

- ■ This clarifies the objection for you.

- ■ It gives you time to think.

- ■ Always end with a question: "Am I correct in assuming that . . . ?" "Is that right?"

3. Isolate the objection.

- ■ Find out if this is the only objection they have.

- ■ Commit to a decision—"If it weren't for that, would you buy the house today?"

4. Show them something that might help them make a decision.

- ■ Discuss builder incentives and comparable values in the market.

- ■ Inform them of financing information that reflects attractive rates and/or terms.

5. *Ask the closing questions.*

- ■ "That makes a difference, doesn't it?"

- ■ "Do you have any more questions?"

The Decision Maker: Agent, Dominant Prospect or Team?

When you show property to your prospects for weeks with no contract in hand, you can begin to feel that there is no decision maker present. The frustration that you feel is equal in intensity to the disappointment your purchasers feel if they are still in the "let's see if there's anything else we need to see before we make a decision" mode. How does this nonproductive cycle end?

It ends when the professional salesperson asks for the order or frankly discusses with the customers their apparent reluctance to make a decision. The toughest job that anyone has is that of making a decision; most people will do anything to avoid the process. If there is no urgency about the purchase, consumers will not be sold until enough positive feelings and facts have been reflected to them about the property, it's location, its features, benefits and financial terms to assure them that they're making a good decision.

To project a positive property picture to the purchaser, teamwork is required . . . repeatedly. As a team, continually *refine* and reidentify the priorities of the purchase—price, features, terms or location. At every significant step in the closing cycle, solicit the input of *all* purchasers. Beware of the silent stomper—the purchaser who never participates in the discussions, but once the decision is made, kicks the sale aside. Equally dangerous is the dominant prospect who demands constant service and is impatient with any input from the spouse or partner. The dominant decision maker often makes a decision impulsively and after careful evaluation will seek to withdraw from the contract. The dominant prospect should be regarded as a quarterback to the transaction. You, however, are the coach who develops the strategy to win the sale.

Teamwork requires that all parties involved in the sale communicate—beginning with the salesperson. Ask qualifying questions and close for the order throughout your presentation. Listen to "Chatty Charlie" and involve "Silent Susie" in every decision to negotiate a sales contract with them. Remain sensitive to the purchasers' roles in the transaction, but involve yourself as the captain of the team that must make a purchasing decision.

Tips on Closing

Closing is the process of guiding the buyer toward making a decision, and then asking for the offer.

It happens throughout the selling process.

■ You guide the prospect toward a decision.

■ You help the prospect to picture the benefits of owning the home.

■ You increase the prospect's involvement by asking questions and then use closes that you feel will be effective in gaining agreement.

Exhibit 6.1 on pages 77-78 supplies you with simple one-line closes, as well as example/explanation closes. Note favorites and use them in your sales presentation.

Choosing the Right Close

All the time you are with the buyers, listen closely and carefully observe behavior. Be attuned to their moods, attitudes and situations. Your approach to closing must fit the buyer. To choose the best closing technique and use it successfully:

■ Watch for buying signals.

■ Relieve buyer tension.

■ Maintain control.

■ Use a trial close.

A few common closing techniques follow. To encourage you to take a personal approach, a few lines have been added, where appropriate, for you to jot down your own ideas.

Assumptive Close—Use when there are no objections.

"When do you need possession? No problem, let's start the paperwork."
Personal Example: _____

_____

_____

Exhibit 6.1   35 Ways To Close

Statistics show that 80 percent of all sales are made after the fifth close. Use one (or five!) of the following techniques to close the sale.

1.   Urgency—inflation

      "In the building industry, as in other industries, costs tend to rise over time. Why not purchase today and stay ahead?"

2.   Urgency—early pricing of homes

      "The pioneers in a community are the homeowners who generally get the lowest prices. Why wait and pay more for the same home?"

3.   Urgency—job starting

      "Would you like to be settled in your new home two weeks or four weeks before your new position begins?"

4.   Urgency—choice of locations

      "This (secluded, scenic view, close to amenities) location is a choice homesite. Let's make sure that you get it for your family."

5.   Urgency—personal to buyer

      "I know you (want to be in by the start of school, like the almond countertops, want to choose your own vinyl colors, want to be in by Christmas), let's be sure you get what you want."

6.   Urgency—general

      "How would you feel if you returned and this house was taken?"

7.   "Let's take it off the market, shall we?"

8.   "Shall we put your name on it?"

9.   "When would you like to move in?"

10.   "How would you like to take title?"

11.   "We've found it, haven't we?"

12.   "Would you kindly put this 'sold' pin on the map?"

13.   "Did you bring your checkbook?"

14.   "When is it convenient to meet with the lender?"

15.   "Would you like to be in before July 1?"

16.   (Handing over the pen:) "Who's the writer in the family?"

Exhibit 6.1 (cont'd)   **35 Ways To Close**

---

17.   "How do you spell your last name?"

18.   (Handing over the pen) "Who'll do the honors and go first?"

19.   "If I can change that (texture, fixture, color), will you go ahead?"

20.   "Shall we pick your colors now?"

21.   "Do you want it?"

22.   Color selection

       "When would you like these installed—by the first or the fifteenth?"

23.   Call for a loan appointment. Set it. Start writing the purchase agreement.

24.   "Let's see how it looks on paper."

25.   "Let's go through the sales agreement so you know how it looks."

26.   "I'd like you to know how this builder makes sure you get quality assurance."

27.   "How much are you prepared to give me as a deposit today?"

28.   Summarize. "Let's review what you like about it again, shall we?"

29.   Barometer close. "Visualize a barometer. Zero means you don't like this home at all; ten means you're ready to put your name on it right now. Where are we on this scale? What would it take to get you to ten at this time?"

30.   "The time to make a decision is when you have all the facts. Is there anything you need to know?"

31.   The prospects say they need to think about it. "This home just won't be here. Let's go take a look at your second choice."

32.   Show the tax advantages of home ownership.

33.   The spouse arrives alone. "Let's write this up subject to your wife's/husband's approval to make sure this one is held for you."

34.   Prestige. "I know you will be proud of this home in our community."

35.   Pull out the paperwork and start writing.

Alternative Choice Close

"Would you like to move in on the 13th or would the 15th be better?"
Personal Example: _____

_____

_____

Empathy Close

The prospect is especially tense—give an example of someone who felt the same way.
Personal Example: _____

_____

_____

Order Blank Close

This process involves using your sales contract as your note pad . . . where you write down all points of agreement. The rationale for using this close is that it's an *orderly* way to record all the information that needs to be reviewed before signing a contract.

Ben Franklin Close

The classic pluses and minuses of the buying decision are recorded.
Personal Example: _____

_____

_____

Competitive Comparison Close

This close allows an opportunity to record what your prospects love about the current home they are seeing and other homes they have seen while shopping. Hopefully the current home will carry the decision.

Be certain that your buyers compare:

- Prices
- Terms of the sale including:
  - Builder incentives
  - Amenities
  - Location
  - Size

Builder Incentives

Your builder has designed a marketing package to sell the product. Builder incentives do help to close the sale. Know them and use them. Some examples are:

- Closing costs

- Appliance package

- Points

- Association fees

- What the builder includes as standard features

Encourage the builder to include several "extras" as standards.

The Closing Cycle

The act of closing the sale is cultivated methodically and renewed constantly as you refine your techniques and sharpen your sensitivities. Join the Major Leagues of Sales . . . ask for the ORDER utilizing the systems and techniques discussed in this chapter.

The chart in Exhibit 6.2 on page 81 summarizes the closing cycle and includes notes and references. Keep it in a convenient place and use it as a reference.

Exhibit 6.2   The Closing Cycle

Please note this straightforward diagram that visually reflects the closing cycle and shows us what to do if we get a "yes" answer or a "no" answer.

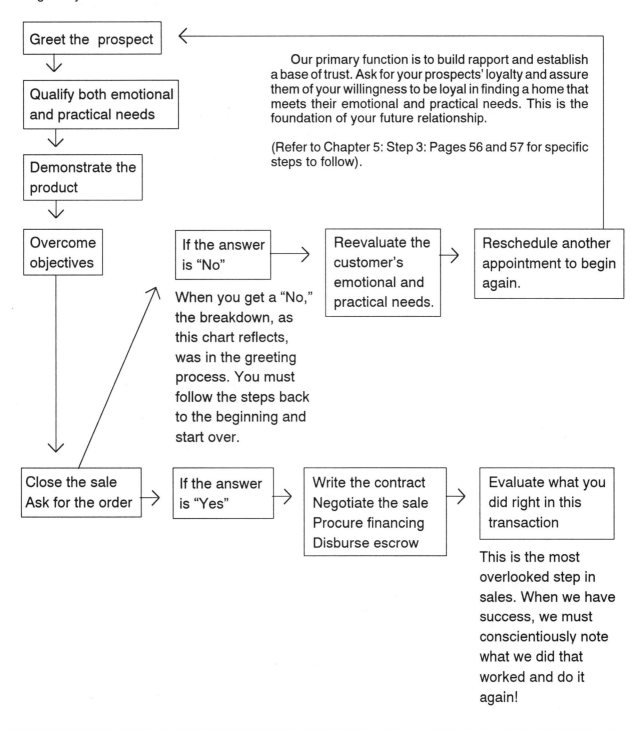

Greet the prospect

Qualify both emotional and practical needs

Demonstrate the product

Overcome objectives

Our primary function is to build rapport and establish a base of trust. Ask for your prospects' loyalty and assure them of your willingness to be loyal in finding a home that meets their emotional and practical needs. This is the foundation of your future relationship.

(Refer to Chapter 5: Step 3: Pages 56 and 57 for specific steps to follow).

If the answer is "No"

When you get a "No," the breakdown, as this chart reflects, was in the greeting process. You must follow the steps back to the beginning and start over.

Reevaluate the customer's emotional and practical needs.

Reschedule another appointment to begin again.

Close the sale
Ask for the order

If the answer is "Yes"

Write the contract
Negotiate the sale
Procure financing
Disburse escrow

Evaluate what you did right in this transaction

This is the most overlooked step in sales. When we have success, we must conscientiously note what we did that worked and do it again!

Capitalizing on Your Follow-Up Services

Follow-up is the glue that holds contracts together until closing and binds relationships with co-broke agents for repeat business and positive personal endorsements of your service in the marketplace. Your attention to follow-up is a reflection of your professionalism and your concern for maintaining a well-informed relationship with all parties to the sale. The best compliment you can get is the knowledge that both your sales peers and purchasers sing your praises in the area of attention to detail and follow-up.

The following systems have proven effective and time-sensitive in many marketplaces throughout this country. If you find a new approach, try it—you might like it!

Keys to Consistent Co-Broke Support

Communication with your co-broke peers is vital to new home sales success. The first "sell" you have to make of your site is to your co-broke REALTOR® community. This can be accomplished by practicing a few simple welcoming and follow-up systems.

1. Warmly welcome your co-brokes—treat them as customers and greet them with a handshake, a smile and a willingness to help them make a sale.

2. Protect their relationship with their customers by reiterating your perspective of their customers and your standard operating procedure of paying sales commission to the co-broke agent.

3. Return co-broke phone calls *promptly*—they may be trying to write a contract.

4. Ask if co-brokes mind if you show the product. Discuss with them (away from the customer) your desire to point out all the community benefits and features as well as to discuss builder incentives.

5. Compliment the co-brokes to their customers.

6. Send thank-you notes within 24 hours of the co-broke's visit and follow up with a phone call within three to five days.

7. Give co-brokes a gift and send a thank-you note when they make a sale at your site.

8. Ask if you may contact their customer, or if they would rather do so if there are any questions during the transaction.

9. Invite area REALTORS® to small onsite broker parties to celebrate the sales they've made at your property. Include them in your real estate company's awards dinners.

10. Make personal visits to other real estate offices to thank the REALTORS® for their support of your site. It never hurts to take a small gift.

11. Get *feedback* . . . from them on your community, your product, your builder and your terms of sale. Let them know their opinions count.

Mining the Gold: Prospect Follow-Up

Prospects are precious in today's overcrowded product market and highly populated real estate agent's arena. With fewer qualified prospects as a result of inflation, prospect follow-up has been redefined. A buyer who five years ago would have been discarded as unqualified and unwilling is now promoted to pending prospect status! He or she has problems that you, as the agent, are trying to solve whether through debt consolidation, letters of explanation for future increases in income, one-time development of income through annual bonus or commissions or letters of explanation to clarify poor past credit histories. Today you have to be flexible enough to seek solutions to any prospect's problems so that you can translate them into purchases. Follow-up is key to this translation. Put your prospects on your follow-up phone list and contact them every 10 to 14 days to determine the progress they've made in solving their problems and renew your offer to help with those problems.

With prospects who simply have not made a buying decision, practice the 3 R's . . .

- Regularly call them to schedule a showing of another property that you feel could capture their interest.

- Reschedule the showing of the home in which they have shown a great deal of interest but just haven't bought yet! Stress that you wish to point out hidden values, construction features or upgrades the builder is willing to negotiate that were not shown on their first visit. It is sometimes helpful to reschedule repeated showings of the same property to the same purchaser with the builder who can usually overcome product objections and answer detailed construction questions.

- Rite (or write) to the prospect *weekly*! Let them know of new sales made, new move-ins, new products that have been started and new amenities that have been planned, started or finished. Mail a site newsletter to them monthly as well as anniversary notes every month after their first visit as pleasant reminders that time and your community are marching on and you want them in your parade.

The follow-up you do today will result in the commission you collect in the future. Figure this out: no follow-up today equals no ___ tomorrow.

The Kid Glove Touch: Buyer Follow-Up after the Sale

Systematic communication with your buyer after the sale results in happy campers on all sides of the transaction. The following represent systematic methods for buyer follow-up:

- Have the buyers complete an Aye and Nay sheet for the builder identifying what they do and don't like about the community and product. Stress the importance of such feedback to the builder. Exhibit 7.1 on page 86 is an Aye and Nay sheet with instructions for its use.

- Call the purchasers weekly to update them on the status of their loan, the construction progress of their home and the status of their closing. In Chapter 8, report forms have been included to facilitate *written* reports of the progress made in these three areas.

Exhibit 7.1   New Homes Buyer Product Input

Aye   Nay

Buyer Signature:

_____

(optional)

_____

Date

Procedure: The purpose of this form is to give consumer feedback to the builder about his or her product. Keep a clipboard pad of these forms in the sales center. After greeting your buyers, give them the clipboard and ask them to record their comments on this form. Invite them to sign their name. If they choose not to sign, please record their name after they leave the site. Turn these in to the New Homes Director weekly for review with your builder!

Exhibit 7.2   Letter 1: Follow-Up to First Visit

Dear _____ ,

Thank you for your interest in Southall Landings on the Bay. We hope you enjoyed your visit to our waterfront homes. We are very proud of our quality construction and are always happy to share our homes with visitors.

If you have any comments or questions about our community, please feel free to call or stop by to talk with us. We look forward to staying in touch and hope to welcome you back to Southall Landings in the very near future.

Sincerely,

Exhibit 7.3   Letter 2: Follow-Up to Second Visit

Dear _____ ,

Thank you for your continued interest in Southall Landings on the Bay. We hope you enjoyed your recent visit with us; it was our pleasure to see you again.

We take pride in what we do. Our commitment to excellence and attention to detail set us apart in a competitive market. Quality living takes superior craftsmanship, comfortable surroundings and people who care to make a house a home. We provide this and more.

Once again, we appreciate your interest in our community and hope to be of service to you. Please call when we can be helpful.

Sincerely,

- If your purchasers live out-of-town, take photos of their house monthly and mail to them.

- Mail any information your purchasers would find enjoyable or helpful about their new community or neighborhood such as arts and crafts schedules, dates and descriptions of area fairs and festivals, children's activity schedules, dance, aerobics, art classes, etc.

- Have the local newspaper sent to them for 30 days prior to their move.

- Offer to provide all information needed to initiate utility services.

- Provide literature on area schools, emergency services and civic and social organizations.

- Give your customers a housewarming gift upon the closing of their sale. Make it personal—and permanent—a framed photo of their new home, a gift related to a family hobby or collection, a handmade gift reflecting their personal taste and preference in housing.

- Remember move-in day with a generous basket of goodies . . .

  - A lunch basket complete with beverages, ice and cups

  - A cleaning basket with cleansers, paper products, brushes, a mop and brooms

  - A personal toiletries basket—toothbrushes for all, toothpaste, bath soap, bath powder, deodorant, hand cream, razors, after shave, a brush, and a comb and barrettes or ponytail holders if there's a little girl (Make your basket special—perhaps a romantic assortment of bath oil, scented candles, wine or champagne, specialt pate, crack ers, cheeses and chocolates and maybe a small bouquet of fresh flow- ers to adorn an otherwise upside down house on moving day.)

- Last, but not least, offer to participate with them in a housewarming party. Express your desire to contribute food, beverages, paper prod- ucts, entertainment or invitations to the party. Let your customers know that you would like to be present to meet their guests and to possibly meet a new prospect for the neighborhood.

In closing, review the sample follow-up letters in Exhibits 7.2 through 7.5 on pages 87 and 89. These can be used with first visit prospects, second visit prospects and broker prospects.

Exhibit 7.4   Letter 3: Alternative Follow-Up to Second Visit

Dear _____ ,

  It was a pleasure to meet with you again. We appreciate your continued interest in our community and look forward to scheduling a time to talk with you further.

  We'll be in touch within the next few days. If you have any questions in the meantime, please do not hesitate to call. Thank you for the opportunity to be of service.

                                Sincerely,

Exhibit 7.5   Letter 4: Co-Broker Follow-Up

Dear _____ ,

  I d like to thank you for taking the time to show our site to your buyer on (insert date).

  We at Southall Landings appreciate your confidence in our product and service and look forward to working with you in the future.

  If you have questions or require additional information, feel free to call or stop by at any time.

                                Sincerely,

The Triple Play: Tracking, Communicating, Reporting

A critical element of your job as sales specialist involves communicating with both the builder and the buyer. This chapter provides a simple system of forms for you to complete and distribute in order to keep the lines of communication open and clear. Each form is accompanied by a procedural statement explaining its use.

Tracking Reports

The following forms can be used in any new home sales environment. Each clearly shows what information is needed and the procedure statements provide clear directions.

Contracts

Procedure: After writing the contract with your buyer at the site, follow these steps:

- If the contract needs the approval of your Broker-In-Charge before you present it to the builder, submit the contract to the broker within 24 hours requesting immediate review.

- *Run an in-house credit report* and highlight any problem areas. Attach this report to the contract to review content with the builder in *general* terms. By law, specific contents may not be revealed to the builder.

Exhibit 8.1   Builder Authorization Form

Material contents delivered: _____

_____

Delivered by: _____

Date: _____

_____

Procedure:

This sign-off sheet, to be used when delivering any items to the builder, provides a written record of delivery. All such forms should be placed in a "Builder's Authorization Receipts" file with the most current form on top. One file should be kept per project. If there is more than one primary person to whom you deliver items, maintain one file per key person or project.

■ Make copies of the financial worksheet, contract and other sales information to give to the builder at the time the contract is signed. Originals will be kept in the site sales office.

■ Have the contract presented to the builder within 24 hours of sale by the site agent or manager (as your in-house procedure stipulates).

■ *Fully signed* contracts are to be copied.

– Originals are to be kept in the Pending Sales file at the broker's main office.

– A sales file should be kept at the site.

– A copy of the contract is to be mailed to the buyer (or co-broke agent if it is a co-broke sale). This can, of course, be hand-delivered if the builder is local.

– A copy is to be delivered to the closing attorney.

Exhibit 8.2   Referral Form from New Homes Department to Relocation Department

Date of Referral _____

Name of Referral _____

Address of Referral _____

_____

_____

Home Phone No. (___) _____   Work Phone No. (___) _____

Listing Referral _____

Listing Agent _____

Selling Referral _____

Selling Agent _____

Referral Fee _____ of _____ Side

(Selling/Listing)

Requested agents to work this referral in order of preference:

1. _____

2. _____

3. _____

Please verify receipt of this referral indicating the name of the person who received the referral and the date of placement.

_____   _____

Relocation Director   Assigned Agent

_____

Date

Procedure:

This form is to be filled out by the site salesperson when working with a buyer who must sell a home before purchasing. This outbound referral is appropriate in new homes sales situations in which the site salesperson is not permitted to list resale properties. This form provides site agents with input to assure optimum service for the seller while also assuring themselves of a high percentage of conversions for greater commission dollars.

Exhibit 8.3 **Weekly Prospecting Report**

Site Name: _____

Agent Name: _____ Month Ending: _____

	Mon.	Tues.	Wed.	Thurs.	Fri.	Sat.	Totals
Telephone							
Door to Door							
Model Event							
Seminars							
Referrals							
Other Broker							

Procedure: This form is to be filled out daily and turned in weekly to the builder and/or broker in charge. Total numbers must be supported with a documented list of names, addresses and telephone numbers, attached to this report.

The purpose of the Prospecting Report is twofold.

1. It daily reflects to you, the agent, prospecting activities that will result in future commission income.

2. It validates to the builder that, daily, you are striving to support any and all of his or her passive prospecting campaigns. This report further ensures your builder loyalty and support when your sales volume slows down whether due to general market conditions or change in the economic climate.

Exhibit 8.4 **Monthly Prospecting Report**

Site Name: _____

Agent Name: _____ Month Ending: _____

	Week Ending ___/___/___	Week Ending ___/___/___	Week Ending ___/___/___	Week Ending ___/___/___	Totals
Telephone					
Door to Door					
Model Event					
Seminars					
Referrals					
Other Broker					

Procedure: This form, to be given to the builder monthly, should reflect monthly totals in each category per week.

Exhibit 8.5   Weekly Activity: New Homes Product Input Report

Community _____ Week Beginning _____ Ending _____

MARKETING

SOURCE	RETURN	REFERRAL	SIGNS / DRIVE BY	NEWS PAPER / RADIO	AGENT PREVIEW	AGENT W/CUST.	TOTAL TRAFFIC	PROSPECTS A	B	C	SALES	CALLS IN / MADE	APPT. SCHED / HELD	MAIL OUT	TOURS / PRES	WEATHER
MONDAY																
TUESDAY																
WEDNESDAY																
THURSDAY																
FRIDAY																
SATURDAY																
SUNDAY																CONV RATE / SLS + TRF
WEEKLY																
YEAR TO DATE																SLS + TRF

SALES

PURCHASER	CONTRACT DATE OF ORIGINATION	MODEL	PRICE	DATE OCCUPANCY DESIRED	REMARKS (i.e. Special Requests Upgrades To Be Installed)

Procedure: Refer to Page 2 of this form for procedure.

Exhibit 8.5 (cont'd)   **Weekly Activity: New Homes Product Input Report**

CANCELLATIONS

PURCHASER	JOB #	MODEL	PRICE	COMMENTS

STATUS

MODEL TYPE	RELEASED	SOLD	BALANCE		CLOSED	OCCUPIED UNCLOSED	APPROVED UNCLOSED	TOTAL SALES	CANCELLED	REMARKS
			COMP.	CONST.						

SETTLEMENT THIS PERIOD   SETTLEMENT ACTIVITY NEXT PERIOD

PURCHASER	ACTIVITY	JOB NO.	PURCHASER	ACTIVITY	JOB NO.

COMMENTS

Procedure: *This single form allows accurate reporting weekly to the builder of prospect/visitor sources, frequency and services rendered. It also reflects sales made, cancellations, status of all inventory, settlements scheduled for this week and settlements scheduled for next week. Complete all sections weekly.*

Exhibit 8.6   Site Consultant Prospecting Log: Summary of Totals

Agent: _____   Community: _____   Date: Month/Week _____

TOTAL OF SOURCES	TOTAL NUMBERS
Completed Appointments	
Walk-Ins	
Sign	
Military Paper Ad	
Model Event	
Friend	
Prospect Letter	
Former Buyer	
Other	
GRAND TOTAL	

Procedure: *This log is to be kept at the site and is to be filled out daily and turned in to the broker-in-charge or New Homes Director by the site manager weekly. These weekly totals per category will be turned in to the builder in a monthly report to document sources of prospects.*

Exhibit 8.7   Site Consultant Prospecting Log: Open Contract Tracking Form

NEW HOME SITE NAME: _____   SITE MANAGER: _____

BUYER	Date of Purchase	Amount of Sales Price	Source of Buyer	Projected Closing Date	Projected Closing/Cost Type of Mortgage	Sales Agent
Name:						
Place of Employment:						
Address:						
Phone:						
Name:						
Place of Employment:						
Address:						
Phone:						
Name:						
Place of Employment:						
Address:						
Phone:						

Procedure: This form is to be filled out each time a contract is written.

Maintain forms at the site in the site notebook and one at the main office in the Monthly Reports Notebook.

Record CLOSED on entries as they close to keep records current. Mark them with a green marker.

Record cancellations by marking them with a black marker.

Record pending sales that will move forward to the next month to close in yellow. Keep these forms in chronological order by dates. At a glance, you can see closing progress, fallout rates and pending activities.

Exhibit 8.8   Financial Information Form

SUBDIVISION NAME: _____

CONTRACT SITE AGENT: _____

Purchaser (s) Name: _____   Date:_____

Property Address: _____

Lot _____, Block _____, Section _____, Closing Attorney _____

SALES PRICE: _____   Options Are: Home Style: _____

(List them here)

TOTAL OPTIONS: _____   1) _____ @_____

2) _____ @_____

TOTAL PRICE: _____   3) _____ @_____

4) _____ @_____

Deposit: _____   Cash Down Payment:_____

Mortgage Amount:_____   (Interest Rate _____%, _____yr.)

Loan Type (Be Specific) _____   Lender: _____

MONTHLY PAYMENT*   **CASH OUTLAY***

Principle/Interest _____   Total Down Payment _____

Real Estate Taxes _____   Closing Costs _____

Private Mortgage Ins. _____   Prepaid Items _____

Homeowners Insurance _____   Total _____

Total Payment _____   Less Deposit _____

Homeowners Assoc. Fee _____   BALANCE DUE AT

(if applicable)   SETTLEMENT _____

CLOSING COST*

LOAN ORIGINATION FEE 1%   _____

LOAN DISCOUNT POINTS— _____ points   _____

CREDIT REPORT   _____

APPRAISAL   _____

SURVEY   _____

TITLE POLICY   _____

RECORDING OF DEED OF BARGAIN & SALE + CLERK'S FEES

_____

ATTORNEY'S FEE   _____

TOTAL   _____

* ALL FIGURES ARE ESTIMATED. APPRAISAL FEE AND CREDIT REPORT FEE DUE AT TIME OF APPLICATION TO LENDER.

_____   _____

PURCHASER   DATE

_____   _____

PURCHASER   DATE

AGENT PREPARED BY _____

Communicating with All Parties

Communication and follow-up are the keys to success in any sales career. New home sales demands a high degree of communication and follow-up—with the builder, the co-broke sales community and the buyers.

Communication with the builder requires statistical reports that document your prospecting and daily site activity, while communication with the buyer demands consistency and simplicity. Procedural directions and simple forms are presented here to help you improve communications with both builders and buyers.

Meetings with the Builder

Since time is money, you are the last person your builder wants to meet with—unless you have a contract in your hand. To respect the builder's time, streamline all meetings through the use of the straightforward reports proposed in this chapter. Review the highlights of each with the builder and leave copies of all reports for their timely review.

Monthly Meetings with the Builder

Procedure: Monthly builder meetings are necessary in order to maintain rapport and identify areas of concern that must be addressed.

Data provided by agent is as follows:

- New Homes Product Input Report

- Monthly Prospecting Report

- Review of the monthly advertising program

- A review of monthly advertising expenses that clarifies who is responsible for the payment of what monies (Beware of committing the broker to heavy advertising costs unless the agreed-to rate of commission allows *ample* monies to fund these campaigns. Advertising is a direct cost of doing business for builders and is typically reflected as such in their business pro formas. REALTOR® participation is ideally limited to the presentation of new home products within the confines of current institutional ads run by the real estate agencies.)

- A review of marketing strategies in progress

- An introduction of new marketing strategies

- A discussion of special marketing promotions

- Comments from prospective home buyers; Aye/Nay sheets

- Comments from other real estate agents

- A review of pending contracts

- A discussion of dates provided by the builder/developer

- A discussion of the length of time remaining before the completion of additional homes

- An update on prices of homes or options to prospective home buyers

- An update on changes of models on remaining homes

- A discussion of future plans for development

- A presentation of any new builder incentives

Procedure:

1. *Schedule this meeting for a specific time, date and location.*

2. *Take a written agenda and make every effort to follow it clearly.*

3. *Allow time to discuss items of concern with the builder.*

4. *Present Aye/Nay Sheets and monthly reporting forms to the builder. (Refer to Chapter 7 for Aye/Nay Sheets.)*

5. *Follow up your builder meetings with personal notes thanking them for their time and input.*

The Meeting Agenda

Fundamentally, an agenda is an outline that helps you to manage time during builder meetings. The following topics need to be included:

- Date of meeting

- Location of meeting

- Persons in attendance

- Topics to be discussed

  – New sales made

  – Closed sales

  – Pending sales

  – Sales Personnel Concerns:

    • Hours of operation

- Supplies needed
- Personnel changes
- Advertising
- Print—Newspaper
- Electronic—TV, Radio, Video (Cover both creative direction of the campaigns and sources for placement. Use the information reflected on your guest registration cards and your New Homes Product Input Report to identify sources for your buyers.)

- Special events planned on site
- Changes in product information
- A review of what the most aggressive competitors are doing
- A discussion of financing
  - Builder incentives to buyer
  - Builder incentives for co-broke agents
  - Builder buydown of mortgage rates
  - Price reductions
  - Price increases
  - Optional features costs
- Other topics (Include any topics the builder wishes to discuss.)

Review the agenda with the builder prior to beginning the meeting. Add the builder's topics and agree on the length of time available to complete your discussion. Exhibit 8.9 on page 103 contains sample minutes from a builder/REALTOR® meeting.

Status Reports

Status reports update the builder weekly on the current position of items that you had previously agreed to handle. They need to be in writing, brief and set up numerically addressing one complete topic per numeral. This report needs to be submitted on the same day each week to provide consistency. This report provides closure for completed assignments. More importantly, it shows the builder that you have not dropped any loose ends while you attend to the hundreds of details involved in operating a new home site. Exhibit 8.10 on page 104 is a sample Status Report.

Exhibit 8.9   Minutes from a Builder/REALTOR® Meeting Re: Southall Landing (March 7,1989)

1. Site plan due to us on March 10, 1989

2. Floor plans due to us on March 10, 1989

3. Perspective rendering due on March 10, 1989

    1-3 confirmed by Orlen March 3, 1989

4. Orlen and Nancy discussed completion of Southall Landing sales center. Goal for installation—April 10, 1989

5. Signage proposal due from Orlen on March 9, 1989

    Directionals

    ■ At entrance in front of monument

    ■ In island at fork in road

    ■ Ground mounted sign at visitor's center with hours of operation. A. B. has to approve signage build-out cost.

6. Determine specific hours of operations

7. Canopy at entrance in copper, from Young Awning for a cost of $750 to $900—includes installation and logo

8. Ad Campaign—discuss and review

9. Special Events, April 12, 1989 date confirmed

    ■ Confirm menu

    ■ Entertainment: Sonny Morris

    ■ Gifts: Rose on day of event

    ■ House Demonstrations: arranging with vendors

    ■ Limo Service: VIP will be quoting prices

10. Note cards and stationery, discuss quote

Exhibit 8.10   Status Report

Community: Southall Landing
From: NDE Impressions Incorporated
To: A. B. Southall, Jr.
Date: March 3, 1989

1. Site map approved March 2, 1989.

2. Rough drawing of perspective approved March 2, 1989.

3. Guest card information submitted to A.B. Southall, Jr. for review.

4. Gene White met with A. B. Southall, Jr. to review property and prepare building construction sales schedule for the 10 AM meeting on Tuesday, March 7, 1989.

5. Brochure copy was delivered for review on March 1, 1989. Amended copy is hereby attached for your review and approval.

6. NDE anticipates delivery of two media proposals on March 3, 1989 and will have for your review on Tuesday.

7. NDE thanks A. B. Southall, Jr. for his approval of brochure proof, photos, layout, foiling and color selection on February 28, 1989.

8. Orlen Stauffer of East Coast Scenic is in the process of ordering chairs for the table in the sales center per Ginny's request of March 2, 1989.

9. Copy of advertising contract from Virginia Business is enclosed.

Thank You for the Opportunity To Serve You!

Understanding the Contract Closing Cycle

Have you ever had a closing in which an item was missing and each person at the closing table—attorney—buyer—agents—couldn't understand why? Usually the missing link is something that everyone present assumed another party to the contract was handling. In an effort to avoid this scenario in your closings, try using this step-by-step operations cycle. Note that each identified cycle stipulates who does what.

The Builder's Responsibilities

The builder is to deliver the following to the attorney:

- A signed release of lien wavers
- A copy of the Certificate of Occupancy
- A signed deed
- Product and homeowner's warranties
- A soil treatment letter from the exterminator
- A record of all items noted during the walk-thru that require correction prior to closing
- Keys to the property
- An owner's operational guide for appliances and climate control units

The Developer's Responsibilities

If the property being closed is owned by the land/community developer or by the builder who is also the developer, the following two items must be supplied by the developer.

- A signed deed transferring the property to the buyers
- Completion of a HUD 1 form if the mortgage used requires the exhibit

The closing attorney prepares these items, processes the developers' authorizations and has the buyer authorize them at the time of closing.

The Buyer's Responsibilities

Buyers rely heavily upon you, the selling agent, to inform them of their role in closing. As that closing date nears, it is imperative that you supply a written list of items the buyer must bring to closing. Review that list with the buyers 24 hours prior to closing and confirm that they have collected all of the items scheduled.

■ The new home sales agent is to call the co-broke agent or buyer with closing costs 24 hours prior to closing to give the exact amount of money needed to close. The mortgage lender will supply this figure.

■ At the time of closing, the buyer is to provide a certified check for all monies due.

■ If special paid-in-full receipts are due at closing, the buyer brings these to the closing. Example: Buyer has to bring to closing a paid receipt for a charge account.

■ The buyer must provide a homeowner's policy and paid-in-full receipt at closing.

Responsibilities of the Builder's Sales Representative

The builder's sales representative and the attorney must manage the following for the closing:

■ Completion of the building and the certificate of occupancy

■ Approval of the loan

■ Acquisition of the loan package from the lender for the closing workup (Frequently the agent is the runner who makes this happen.)

■ Acquisition of a copy of the title binder from the lender

■ Getting keys from the site manager

■ The new home agent is to provide the following to the attorney:

– Charges outside of the contract (options) to be paid at closing

– Statements of the amount of dollars in escrow

– The change order information that necessitates a collection of funds—when a buyer procures an option late in the transaction

■ The new home salesperson is to:

  – complete a walk-thru with the buyer and the builder's representative and attend the closing on the seller's behalf;

  – attend the closing at the attorney's office, arriving 1/2 hour early to review the closing statement;

  – pick up a check within 24 hours after closing.

New Home Change Orders

Follow these steps for new home change orders:

- All changes must be in writing and signed by the builder and the purchaser.

- The change order must reflect the cost impact on the purchase price.

- Charge a fee of $25 per change order. (Check to confirm that this is acceptable in your company.)

- All change orders must be processed through the site agent, to the New Homes Director, to take pressure off the builder. Once internally approved, the change is submitted to the builder.

- Number change orders to identify the number of changes per contract.

- The builder retains the right to limit the number of change orders.

A change order—typically a change in the amount of money the buyer must pay—occurs after a sales contract has been fully authorized. It is important to note the cost of the change being ordered and who is to absorb it. As an example, at the time of contract, the buyers ordered a $150 ceiling fan for each of the four bedrooms, for a total of $600 to be financed in the total cost of the home. Now, the buyers are ordering a change; they want no ceiling fans, thus saving $600. This change needs to be given to the lender immediately and will necessitate an addendum to the contract.

Since the buyers are not ordering the installation of four ceiling fans at a cost of $600, the change order needs to reflect that either the buyers have added $600 to their funds in escrow or that these funds are to be collected at closing by the attorney.

Operational Walk-Thru Inspection

The site manager or site agent representative needs to walk through the property with the builder or builder representative one or two weeks prior to closing in order to identify any problem areas. The power should be turned on so that all of the home's appliances, lights and climate control systems can be demonstrated.

The walk-thru with the purchasers needs to occur within a week of closing. This should be an instructional session to show the purchaser the water cut-off, the hot water heater controls and the thermostat features. All appliances should be tested and windows, the security system, the intercom, the central air systems, the whirlpool and any additional luxury or convenience features should be demonstrated.

1. The operational checklist is to be used to control the walk-thru.

2. The walk-thru is to be attended by the purchasers, the realty representative and the builder or builder representative.

3. The builder is to instruct the realty representative to be of assistance should the builder be limited in time or unavailable for the walk-thru.

4. The "Operational Checklist" is to have a brief area at the bottom for other comments that may be documented, i.e. punch list itemization of required repairs.

5. The operational checklist is to be signed and dated by the purchaser and the builder.

6. The purchasers are to be given leftover paint for touch up purposes.

7. The purchasers are to be given a "Homeowner's Notebook" with a list of subcontractors to contact if problems arise.

8. The purchasers are advised at walk-thru that they will be permitted one punch list to be submitted to the site agent in 30 days. Any items that need to be documented prior to that must be put on the operational checklist. All paint touch ups not noted on the report will be the responsibility of the purchaser.

9. For this procedure to work, it is imperative that the builder have the house ready for possession (including final touch ups and cleaning). If the house is not ready, *do not* walk through.

Follow all of these procedures carefully to avoid future disappointments. Exhibit 8.11 on page 109 contains a sample operational checklist form.

Exhibit 8.11   Operational Checklist

Subdivision: _____

Legal: _____

Purchaser: _____

1. Foyer—

_____ Overhead Light

_____ Outlets

_____ Door Closes and Lock Operates Properly

_____ _____

_____ _____

2. Living Room—

_____ Outlets

_____ Windows

_____ _____

_____ _____

3. Dining Room—

_____ Overhead Light

_____ Outlets

_____ Windows

_____ _____

_____ _____

4. Family Room—

_____ Outlets

_____ Lighting and Ceiling Fans, if applicable

_____ Windows

_____ Doors and Exterior Locks

_____ _____

_____ _____

5. Staircase, Upstairs Hallway—

_____ Lights

_____ Outlets, if applicable

_____ Pull Down Attic Storage

_____ _____

_____ _____

6. Bath—	1/2	Master	Hall
Windows	____	____	____
Faucets in Sink & Tub/Shower	____	____	____
Outlets & Lights	____	____	____
Toilets	____	____	____

7. Bedrooms—	Master	2	3	4
Outlets & Lights	____	____	____	____
Windows & Screens	____	____	____	____

_____ _____

_____ _____

Exhibit 8.11 (cont'd)   Operational Checklist

8.   Kitchen—
_____ Windows
_____ Faucets
_____ Disposal—Warranty Papers
_____ Dishwasher—Run through Cycles, Warranty Papers
_____ Range—All Heating Elements, Oven(s) and Broiler
                      Warranty Papers
_____ Over Range Exhaust Fan
_____ Lights, Switches, Outlets

_____ _____
_____ _____

9.   Utility Room—
_____ Breaker Box, Main Breaker
_____ Doors and Locks
_____ Hot Water Heater, Warranty Papers, Thermostat
_____ Water Cut-Off Valve
_____ Washer and Dryer Hook-Ups

_____ _____
_____ _____

10. Other—
_____ Turn on Heat in Winter, Cool in Summer To Test Heating System
_____ Instructions on Care of Hardwood Floors
_____ Instructions on Care of Vinyl Floors

_____ _____
_____ _____

11. Outside—
_____ Outside Trap Door Under House
_____ Under House Vents/Open & Close
_____ Heat Pump/Main Electric Switch
_____ Main Electrical Line/Electrical Meter
_____ Exterior Light Fixtures
_____ Water/Sewer Meter

_____ _____
_____ _____

12. Miscellaneous—

_____
_____
_____
_____

Procedure:
    Fill this form out at the time of the walk-thru.
    Have all parties sign it.
    Provide copies for the builder, buyer, closing attorney and office files, both site and main office .
    Be certain the walk-thru is a **positive** *opportunity to demonstrate the product.*

Procedure for Punch List

The punch list documents the changes and repairs deemed necessary after the operational walk-thru.

- The goal of the builder and the realty representative is to eliminate the need for the punch list and mutually attempt to have the property in turnkey condition at the time of the operational walk-thru.

- At the bottom of the operational checklist, the purchaser and the builder document areas of mutual concern that need to be corrected.

- The purchaser is permitted to submit one final punch list to the builder by way of the realty representative 30 days after the closing.

- The builder agrees to complete the final punch list within 30 days of the date received or advise the purchaser in writing, with a copy to the REALTOR® if there will be a delay.

- If the purchaser submits more than one punch list, the builder is only obligated to recognize one. Therefore, it is to the purchaser's advantage to submit one complete list.

- This final list does not replace normal structural builder warranties.

Reporting Forms

The progress of the loan application, new home construction and the scheduled closing is of great interest to all parties concerned—the agent (co-broke if one is involved), the builder and the buyer. Responsibility for reporting progress becomes a little easier if you follow the three forms proposed in this chapter. Tested over time, these forms have proven invaluable in keeping loans on track, construction on schedule with coordination between selling agent and builder and finally, keeping the closing together. The accompanying forms are brief and concise with succinct procedural explanations.

Loan Status Reports

These reports inform buyers *in writing* of their loan status with additional exhibit items as needed. Note the simplicity of the procedural steps.

Exhibit 8.12   Loan Status Report

Memo Update for:

Site Name

Buyer's Name

Purchase Address

Date of Update:
New Homes Manager:
Lender:

1. _____ Date _____
   Loan Package Being Prepared

2.
   Loan Package needs additional exhibit items
   (List items here—be clear in identifying these.)

3.
   Loan is at underwriting

4.
Loan has returned from underwriting BUT additional exhibit items are required:

5.
   Loan Approved

6.
   Additional Comments:

Be certain that your comments give clear, specific information to the BUYER. If requesting additional loan exhibits, give the exact times these are needed.

_____   _____
Site Manager   New Homes Director

_____   _____
Date   Date

Procedure:
(Make 3 copies)   *The original loan status report stays in the main office file.*
1 for the buyer   *Mail these copies on the same day of each **week**.*
1 for the sales agent
1 for the site file

Construction Status Reports

No closing can occur without a completed product. You are encouraged to work cooperatively with the builder and the site superintendent to assure that the product is delivered on time. Thirty days prior to the scheduled closing, initiate a weekly inspection of the property to be completed on the same day of each week and forwarded to all parties involved. The construction status update—Exhibit 8.13—should be sent to the buyer weekly for four weeks prior to closing.

Weekly Physical Inspections of New Homes

The following inspection procedure should be followed at the sites:

- Use the attached Construction Status Report (Exhibit 8.14) to record completion status of each category listed for a multifamily community.

- Homes scheduled to close within each calendar month shall be inspected each Monday between 9:00 A.M. and noon beginning 30 days prior to the closing date. (Note that Monday is the ideal day, since the builder then has the week to complete unfinished items.)
    - If six units are scheduled to close prior to February 28th, those homes would appear on the weekly inspection reports from the last week of January through the month of February.

- Complete one inspection sheet per *building*.
    - Thus, if six homes were to close with three in Building II and three in Building III, *TWO* forms would be turned in—one for Building II, and one for Building III.

- Physical Inspection Reports are due to the builder and the broker-in-charge on Monday.

- A copy of this report is to be delivered by the site manager to the builder's representative with a sign-off sheet signed by the representative prior to the close of business on the day of receipt.

- A copy of this report is to be kept at the site.

- The master report will be kept at New Homes Department Administrative offices or the office of the broker-in-charge, if this is applicable to your operation.

Exhibit 8.13   Construction Status Update

Memo Update for:

_____
Site Name

_____
Buyer's Name

_____
Purchase Address

Date of Update:_____

New Homes Manager: _____

Effective Date:

The Construction Status Update is our way of keeping you informed of progress in the construction of your new home. We urge you to make an appointment with the Site Manager to physically inspect this home 30 days prior to closing. ***This update report will begin 30 days prior to the projected contract closing date so that you and the selling agent can have firsthand knowledge about the status of construction.***

Construction Status Update	Date
1. Building Exterior Status Update	
2. Building Interior Roughed-In	
3. Mechanicals Roughed-In	
4. Building Interior: a. Cabinets Installed b. Countertops Mounted c. Trim Mouldings Completed d. Painting Complete e. Fixtures (Bath) Installed f. Lights Installed g. Carpet Installed h. Appliances Installed	
5. Projected Date for Completion of Home	
6. Scheduled Date of Walk-Thru	

_____   _____
Site Manager   New Homes Director

_____   _____
Date   Date

Exhibit 8.14   Construction Status Report

Subdivision: _____

Record the date of inspection in each block indicating completion of topic.

Topic										
Unit Address										
Projected Closing										
Sheetrock Completed										
Air Conditioning										
Gas Meter										
Furnace										
Stairs										
Water Meter										
Plumbing/Toilets										
Electric Fixtures										
Wood Stain										
Trim Installed										
Cabinets Installed										
Vinyl										
Appliances										
Entrance										
Landscaping										
Carpet										
Cleanup										
Paint										
Walk-Thru										

Date _____ Name _____   Date _____ Name _____

_____   _____   _____   _____

Closing Status Report

When the lender notifies you that the loan has been approved, it is appropriate to complete this closing update (Exhibit 8.15) and distribute it to the builder, the buyer and the attorney. You will need to coordinate the time of closing with both the attorney and the buyer. Your lender must also confirm the ability to *fund* this closing at the scheduled time. The use of this form alleviates misunderstandings at a time in the transaction that is highly charged for everyone. Add it to your bag of buyer services and watch the happy response.

Exhibit 8.15   New Homes Department: Closing Status Report

Memo Update for:

_____
Site Name

_____
Buyer's Name

_____
Purchase Address

Date of Update: _____

New Homes Manager: _____

Effective Date: _____

Projected Closing Date: _____

1. Closing Attorney: _____
2. Loan Package Delivered to Attorney: _____
3. Time of Closing: _____
4. Additional items needed from buyer and/or selling agent for closing:

_____

(Be specific particularly if you are recording funds needed to close and identify the method of payment: Certified funds, etc.)

_____

5. URGENT ITEMS: Please phone the New Homes Site Manager with your response IMMEDIATELY upon receipt of this update.

_____

(This is requested to confirm receipt of this information. Be sure to mail this form promptly to allow time for receipt prior to closing.)

6. Loan Approval Expiration: _____

_____   _____
Site Manager   New Homes Director

_____   _____
Date   Date

Sales Techniques for Lot Sales

Lot sales comprise an intricate part of any project's development process. Lots have to be moved in a timely fashion and an orderly manner to create the need for homes and a completely developed project. This chapter provides a very general approach to selling lots.

■ *Size, Price Range and Lot Layout*

These three areas are usually predetermined by the developer from the master plan of the project. Salespeople should have a general knowledge of range sizes—square footage or percentage of an acre since people like to talk about how much yard space will be available around their home. Price ranges should be quoted in general, from mid-20s, 30s, etc., until your customers are ready to talk specifics about a particular lot that you and they have in mind. Lot layouts should be discussed when you have an indication that your customer has picked out "the special one." The plat of lots you are selling should be part of your itinerary for reference and a source of information because the sale *you will make* depends upon how knowledgeable you are about your customers' wants and needs.

■ *Builder's Specials*

Be aware of the lots that different builders have chosen to build their special homes on and be well versed as to which floor plan will go on which lot. Most builders pick out the lots they feel will be better adapted to their floor plans and overall building scheme. Get the builders to share with you information about decisions on their lots. Many sales can be attributed to the fact that the builder had a pre-arranged plan to fit on a particular lot. Your customers are able to make minor modifications, save time and money and still have the home of their dreams on one of the better lots.

■ *Lot Release Program*

Some people are guilty of selling themselves out of business. It is a good feeling to have an inventory of 20 to 30 lots and within a month be SOLD OUT—counting your commission checks—planning a trip—buying a new car—when a customer appears and wants to buy a lot. You have done a wonderful job. What do you do and say now? You SELL!

You might answer:

–"I'll take a reservation check."

–"I'll take a back-up contract."

–"I'll take your name and call you when more lots come on the market."

The ideal situation is to have inventory that the builder/developer can make available to you and the public on a demand basis—ensuring the urgency factor of buying now. A *planned lot release program* keeps sales and inventory on a smooth path from inception to final development.

■ *Knowledge about Available Inventory and How To Present It*

Always have an inventory list—updated daily or weekly—of available product. This impresses your customer that you are selling on a regular basis. Your approach to clients should indicate that lots are selling at a good pace and your inventory of the most desirable locations at a fair price needs their attention as soon as possible. This is a nice way of saying if you don't buy today, it will be gone the next time you come back.

A Positive Strategy for Lot Releases

Most developer/builders create situations where different parts of the development are released in phases. Supply and demand are factors you can use as sales tools if the buyers can be convinced that they're getting the *best lot at the best price* in this particular release. Most sellers and buyers are comfortable with a percentage of sales price increase in a modest time frame if you can convince them in a logical manner. A successful salesperson will have knowledge about such increases from past and future sales.

Creating That Ideal Mix of Homes and Vacant Lots

During the question and answer process, it's important to determine if the customer desires neighbors or would be more comfortable on a lot next to people who are not planning to build in the immediate future—one at the end of a cul-de-sac or one backing up to a green area. The ideal mix of homes and lots will be determined by you under the influence of the developer/ builder. This concept helps you to qualify buyers and give your customers the feeling that you are looking out for their best interests.

Selecting the "Best Lot" for Your Customer

This process takes a selling job that you have to do on yourself. Pick out the lot that you would buy yourself and sell yourself on all of its features. Know the lot like your own backyard. You have just made your job a lot easier because you have picked out "the best lot" for yourself. Then you must qualify your prospect for need, time and price range.

- Need—Your conversation with customers should center around how many bedrooms, baths and other items they expect to have in their home *when* they build.

- Time—Knowing what they need, when they expect to build, and about how much they can afford for a home will be of benefit to you in helping your customers pick a lot in the affordable range.

- Price Range—Price range of the lots will vary. Customers will usually buy a lot *that you sell them*. Use the qualifying process you are comfortable with to determine the customers' price range. Several "sales pitches" need to be developed to be used as the occasion presents itself.

- Make sure you are knowledgeable about home sizes in relationship to lot sizes with setbacks and zoning restrictions. Becoming familiar with frontage, side and rear lot lines will allow you to discuss different aspects of building with your customers, helping you to make the sale.

- Develop the art of dream-building a home on a particular configuration of lots—level; drop-off; view of what? People who do not desire a basement usually pick a level, flat lot. Some customers prefer a basement and certain lots with a 6- to 10-foot drop on the rear or side are ideal lots for basements or split levels with minimum grading. Become familiar with the views from all angles of the lot; knowing the east-west placement of the house will be very beneficial in your sales presentation. Determine if your customers plan to use passive solar and if so, point out the southerly exposure.

The Art of Walking the Lot

More lots are sold by physically walking the ground than by pointing them out from the car. Knowledge of pin placements, tree count, views of water and proximity to amenities are key points in your presentation. Know the topography of the lots and walk your prospect to the ideal vantage points for them to visualize their home and views.

If you are selling prestige lots that are heavily wooded, ask a botany class from a local college to identify the primary trees on the best lots. Use this information to make your sale. Walk the front line so the customer knows the way the lot faces. Schedule lot walks when buyers are dressed appropriately, the weather is cooperating and you have the community plat map available.

- How can you create your own urgency? If you have asked the right questions, shown the right lots and your customer is showing some interest—the urgency factor of buying now should be approached. If the lot is "one of a kind" and your customer agrees—the sale is made.

- When and how do you ask for a close and contract? *When* you ask for a close will depend on your presentation. Experience teaches you to determine who holds the purse strings and how to direct contract talk to that person. Always ask for a check.

Signs or No Signs?

Following are a few of the primary points to consider when developing a signage package for lots to sell.

- Signs on each lot tell all visitors specifically what you have to sell. Why do they need to call an agent, particularly if the price is on the sign?

- Signs on every lot give the competition an easy way to track future sales.

- Attractive signs at the entrance to the area are imperative to direct buyer interest.

- Avoid detailed signs at an underdeveloped community. Plat maps reproduced on large signs lack warmth and typically confuse the buyer.

- Utilize informational signs when selling lots including:

  - Directional signs from main arteries of traffic to your site

  - A major entry sign to attract immediate attention and recognition

  - Onsite directional signs to point out areas in which lots are for sale and the location of a site sales office

- Provide an informational sign that furnishes a telephone number, name and office address for buyers to visit or call if they're interested in purchasing a lot.

- Use signs to indicate the future site of amenities such as: clubhouse, pool, tennis courts, park and jogging, biking or walking paths.

Overcoming Objections

Be alert when showing lots; if your customers don't like particular features, try to switch them quickly to another lot that doesn't have the same objections. A quick qualifying question would be: "If I could find you a lot without your objections, would you buy today?"

Listen to your customer and if you can, make some minor concessions. Tell them you will try to get some things done if they will sign a contract and put their concessions in writing. A driveway, a few trees cut, a little landscaping and a little imagination on your part, as well as knowing what the developer/builder will go along with, will put money in your pocket.

- Example: 1. Least Expensive

  2. Views

  3. Waterfront or Choice

- Lot Specifics

  - Park your automobile at the corner of the lot stake.

  - Involve your customer in the lot presentation.

  - Dream-build a house/driveway, placement of landscaping, a discussion of what the community will be like upon completion.

- Progressive "Sale-Up" of next two lots

  - The second and third lot presentations should be followed exactly like the first lot preview.

- Your clients will become comfortable if they are involved with walking the lots and making a few decisions. Your presentation should always be geared to leading the clients toward making a buying decision.

■ Return to the office

- Ask your clients which lot they prefer.

- Answer any questions; be specific and logical.

- Talk contracts and explain deposits.

- Pull office files containing inventory and discuss.

- When appropriate, give your clients time to discuss their choice in private. Offer them a beverage while they talk.

- The down payment and monthly outlays should become a vital part of your conversation.

■ Key factors for your success

- A clean car, clean office and appropriate dress

- Tools of the trade (Plats, information, camera and 100' tape help in lot sales—so does a four-wheel drive vehicle.)

- An orderly presentation with *you* in charge

- Asking for the check after proper qualification

- A well designed follow-up program will make additional sales if you follow a logical plan. Staying in touch with your customers with a genuine interest in them brings you many rewards.

Lot Deposit Procedure

■ Establish with the developer a minimum deposit to be accepted, make it nonrefundable and have the realty company or the builder hold it in escrow.

■ The lot deposit should be for a short period of time—two weeks are recommended; 30 days provide time to clarify prices, design, and feasibility per attachments to the lot deposit.

■ This nonrefundable deposit is to cover the builder's expenses of drawing and price changing prices for this specific purchase.

■ See Exhibit 9.1, on page 125, a sample lot deposit agreement.

Exhibit 9.1   Lot Deposit Form

Received from _____ a deposit of $_____

made payable to (your company name) to be applied as part payment of Lot _____, Block _____,

Section _____ , Subdivision _____ .

Home style to be built _____

Projected purchase price _____

Deposit amount to be:

    A. $500 for current floor plans

    B. $1,000 plus builder expenses (approximately $1,500 billable to the purchaser) for custom plans.

The undersigned Purchaser agrees to execute a formal Purchase Agreement by _____ ,

19___. The aforementioned terms of the lot deposit agreement shall automatically become null and void and

deposit shall be paid to the Builder if the Purchaser elects not to contract for the purchase by

_____ , 19___ .

_____   _____

Purchaser   Builder

_____   _____

Purchaser   Builder Representative

_____   _____

Date   Date

_____

Agent on Site

10

New Home Product Knowledge: A Construction Profile

Two primary skills will help you succeed in the field of New Home Sales:

- The ability to talk the builder's language and understand technical information through strong product knowledge

- The ability to present your personalized marketing plan to the builder

The first skill involves a thorough understanding of the New Home product. The New Home Product Profile questionnaire has been designed to teach you the questions to ask builders about their products and to give you an understanding of the product information you need to receive in their answers. This information helps you determine if you can sell the product. Is it compatible with your buyer demand areas? Is the builder offering the quality construction that you would feel comfortable selling?

When you introduce the New Home Product Profile to builders, it is imperative that they understand the importance of their answers. This information will help you create what you feel is the best marketing strategy for their community and will also be used to train the onsite agents who will be responsible for selling the community.

As you go through the questions on the profile sheet, you will see that many of them are similar to those periodically asked of the sales agent by a purchaser. Certain questions may need to be added or deleted, depending upon your marketplace, your builder and your product.

As you read and study the profiles on the following pages, create an image of yourself in a builder's office asking questions and looking for answers such as those listed in this profile. The notes are designed to give you information that you need to know about each question. Marginal notes contain the specific construction information that needs to be integrated into your presentation. Questions on the left hand side of every page are those to be asked of the builder. You may find it helpful to copy the entire profile and use it in all of your builder interviews.

Floor Systems

The identification of components of the home starts with the placement of a sill plate on top of the foundation wall to which the floor system attaches. The four primary types of construction in this country are:

1. *Stick building* involves having every piece of framing measured, cut and constructed onsite.

2. *Pre-cut homes* are measured and cut in a factory controlled environment and delivered in bundles with a master plan for site assembly.

3. *Pre-fabricated construction* identifies sections of the home such as wall panels, floor and roof trusses and built-in cabinets that are constructed in a controlled factory environment and then shipped to the site for assembly. Wall panels are available in open wall (open walls feature studs, prewiring, insulation and exterior sheathing; however, no sheetrock has been applied to the interior of the wall) or closed wall (closed walls include all items listed in the open wall system plus the application of sheetrock to the studs; this wall simply has to be mounted in place to be complete). The advantage of this system is time savings and therefore, cost savings in the life of the job.

4. *Modular construction* designates the assembly of entire sections of a home in a controlled environment with subsequent shipment of these sections to the site for assembly. Assembly typically requires a crane for placement. These modular units have all finish materials included such as carpet, wallpaper, cabinets and kitchen and bath flooring.

Floor framing is designed to provide horizontal support for the load of the house, to insure future stability of the structure and to eliminate vibrations while acting to control sound transmission from area to area.

Refer to Exhibits 10.4 and 10.5 on pages 133-136 for more information.

Exhibit 10.1   Builder Profile

Ask the builder to answer each question as thoroughly as possible, including brand names where applicable.

1. Company Name
   a. List any information that outlines the history of your company. Be as specific as possible.
      1. Official company name
         ■
      2. When was the company established?
         ■
      3. Where was the company established?
         ■
      4. Location(s)
         ■
      5. Who comprises your support staff?
         ■
         ■

         ■

         ■
         ■
      6. What type of homes do you construct?
      7. List several communities you have developed during the past five years.
      8. Are you a HOW (Home Owner's Warranty) builder? If not, what warranty programs do you offer?
      9. Who in your company is responsible for signing contracts?

      10. List any other information you feel is important for us to know about your company.

NOTE:	Be aware that the name on the sign is not the corporate name.
NOTE:	Procure specific street addresses.
NOTE:	Site Superintendent
NOTE:	Architect or Draftsman on staff that makes customizing floor plans a master process for the salesperson
NOTE:	Full-time secretary for easier access to the builder and simplification of administrative processing
NOTE:	Full-time punch list technician
NOTE:	Full-time pricing specialist or estimator
NOTE:	Single family, multi-family, upscale/ luxury, first-time buyer, traditional, contemporary, transitional ranch
NOTE:	If the builder responds that it's only him or her, ask what procedure you follow when he or she is unavailable or out of town. Stress the need for timely authorization of new contracts!
NOTE:	Special recognition received— Builder of the Year Awards, Design Awards, Landscaping Awards, Community Service Awards.

Exhibit 10.2   Foundation System Profile

Ask the builder to describe the complete foundation system that will be used. Exhibit 10.3 depicts the universal types of foundations.

The foundation wall with its footings, which provides support for the entire structure, must extend below the frost line to prevent future cracking and instability.

1.   Description of the foundation

NOTE: Type of materials typically used:

- Brick

- Block

- Poured concrete

- Wire reinforced concrete, etc.

2.   Advantages:

NOTE: Size of footers

- Depth and width (In normal soil the depth is equal to the width.)

- Very cold climates dramatically modify this approach.

3.   Disadvantages:

NOTE: The biggest disadvantage is when a foundation system is not accepted in the community. This decision slows and complicates the sales process.

Refer to Exhibit 10.3 for clarification and explanation in the contrasting systems used in basements, crawl spaces and on grade slabs.

Exhibit 10.3   Foundation Systems

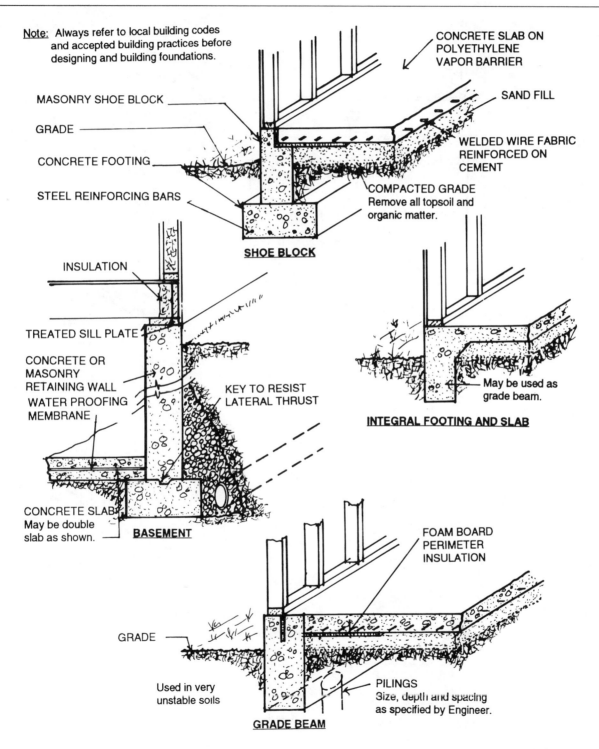

Note: Always refer to local building codes and accepted building practices before designing and building foundations.

MASONRY SHOE BLOCK

GRADE

CONCRETE FOOTING

STEEL REINFORCING BARS

CONCRETE SLAB ON POLYETHYLENE VAPOR BARRIER

SAND FILL

WELDED WIRE FABRIC REINFORCED ON CEMENT

COMPACTED GRADE
Remove all topsoil and organic matter.

SHOE BLOCK

INSULATION

TREATED SILL PLATE

CONCRETE OR MASONRY RETAINING WALL

WATER PROOFING MEMBRANE

KEY TO RESIST LATERAL THRUST

May be used as grade beam.

INTEGRAL FOOTING AND SLAB

CONCRETE SLAB
May be double slab as shown.

BASEMENT

FOAM BOARD PERIMETER INSULATION

GRADE

Used in very unstable soils

PILINGS
Size, depth and spacing as specified by Engineer.

GRADE BEAM

**FOUNDATION SYSTEMS-
CONCRETE SLABS**

Exhibit 10.3 (cont'd)   Foundation Systems

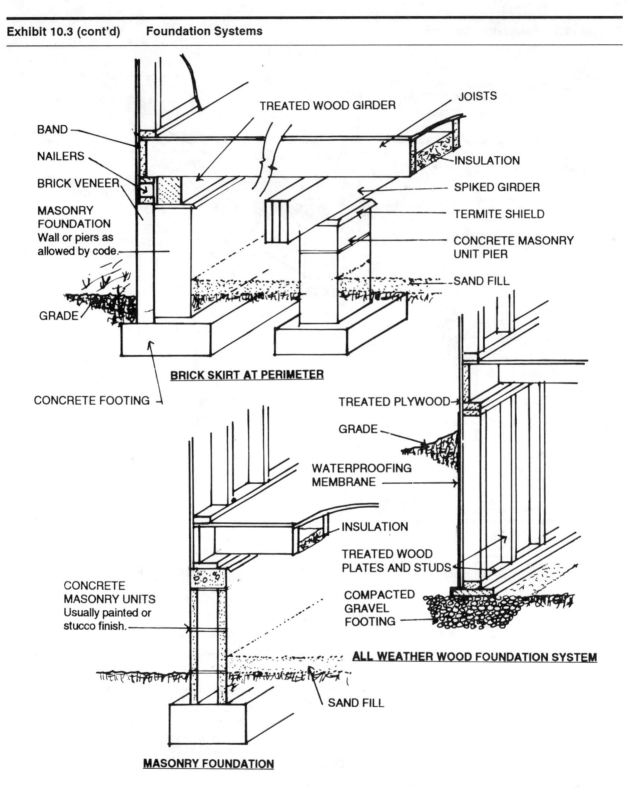

BAND

NAILERS

BRICK VENEER

MASONRY
FOUNDATION
Wall or piers as
allowed by code.

GRADE

TREATED WOOD GIRDER

JOISTS

INSULATION

SPIKED GIRDER

TERMITE SHIELD

CONCRETE MASONRY
UNIT PIER

SAND FILL

BRICK SKIRT AT PERIMETER

CONCRETE FOOTING

TREATED PLYWOOD

GRADE

WATERPROOFING
MEMBRANE

INSULATION

TREATED WOOD
PLATES AND STUDS

COMPACTED
GRAVEL
FOOTING

ALL WEATHER WOOD FOUNDATION SYSTEM

CONCRETE
MASONRY UNITS
Usually painted or
stucco finish.

SAND FILL

MASONRY FOUNDATION

**FOUNDATION SYSTEMS-
CRAWL SPACES**

Exhibit 10.4   Floor System Profile

1. Description of the floor system:

   NOTE: Universal system

      1. Truss system (manufactured support structures)

      2. Joists system (solid wood joists cut onsite, mounted on the foundation and enclosed by the sillband)

2. Description of application of sheathing:

   NOTE: Discuss the floor and decking.

      ■ Type: Usually it's plywood.

      ■ Ask size—1/2", 3/4".

      ■ Ask if it is tongue and groove for tighter fit.

   NOTE: Application of decking is usually one of three types:

      ■ Glued

      ■ Nailed

      ■ Tongue and groove to delete squeaks, sags and buckles in the future

Refer to Exhibit 10.5 which illustrates joists, floor systems, truss system and a cross section of the completed floor decking. Note labels of components for easy self-instruction to utilize in your sales presentation.

The Wall System

The basic parts of the frame wall are the vertical members called *studs*, the top horizontal framing member called the *header* and the bottom horizontal member called the *sole plate*. To remember the key wall components, simply recall that a stud stands upright secured on top by the header and resting on a foundation called the sole plate—much like the human body with a head on top and soles on the bottom.

Conventional construction uses 2"x 4" studs with 16" spacing that is commonly referred to as 16" on centers. This spacing can vary to 24" on center with a change in the size, grade and species of the stud wood or a

Exhibit 10.5   Floor Systems

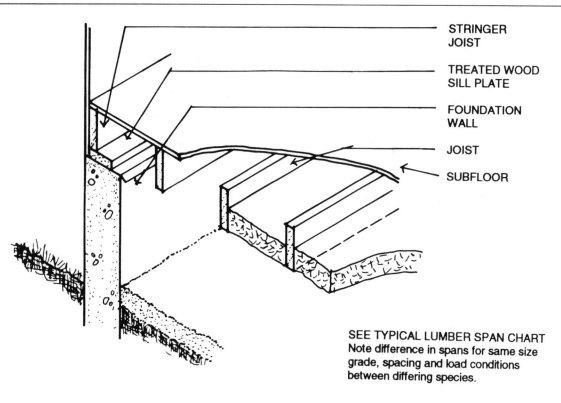

STRINGER
JOIST

TREATED WOOD
SILL PLATE

FOUNDATION
WALL

JOIST

SUBFLOOR

SEE TYPICAL LUMBER SPAN CHART
Note difference in spans for same size
grade, spacing and load conditions
between differing species.

<u>**JOISTS PARALLEL TO WALL**</u>

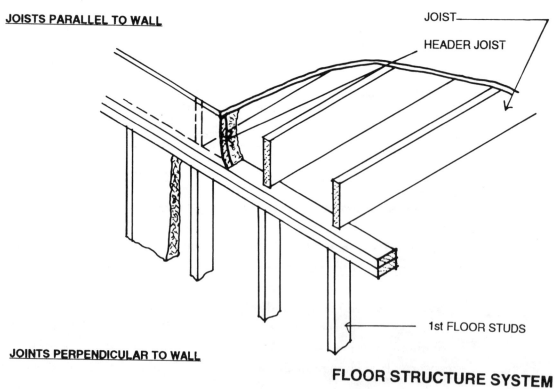

JOIST

HEADER JOIST

1st FLOOR STUDS

<u>**JOINTS PERPENDICULAR TO WALL**</u>

FLOOR STRUCTURE SYSTEM

Exhibit 10.5 (cont'd)   Floor Systems

UNDERLAYMENT
Particle board, fiberboard, etc.

SUBFLOOR
Thickness varies according to spaces, grade and joist.
Spacing indicated by grade stamp on surface of plywood.
May also be particle board.

Plywood laid onto joists with long
dimension perpendicular to joists.

INSULATION

PLYWOOD SUBFLOOR WITH UNDERLAYMENT

APA
RATED STURD-I-FLOOR
20 oc 19/32 INCH
SIZED FOR SPACING
T&G NET WIDTH 47-1/2
EXPOSURE 1
000
NRB-108

A.P.A. GRADE MARK

Single layer construction.

Plywood glued to joists.
Gluing plywood to joists can increase
floor stiffness up to 70%.

2" Blocking between supports unless
tongue and groove plywood is used.

Plywood should be underlayment
grade 19/32" to 1" thick
depending on span (see chart).

Joist spacing at
12", 16", 19.2" or 24" o.c.

GLUED SUBFLOOR / UNDERLAYMENT

FLOOR SYSTEMS

Exhibit 10.5 (cont'd)   Floor Systems

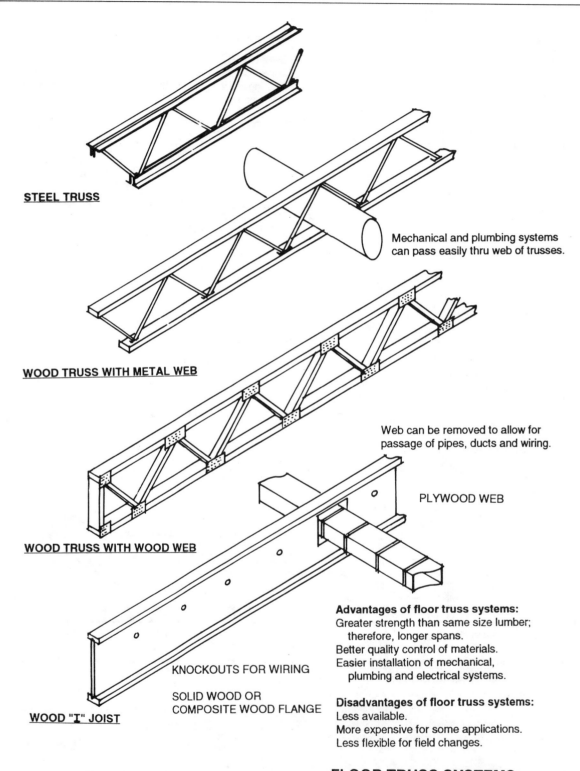

STEEL TRUSS

Mechanical and plumbing systems can pass easily thru web of trusses.

WOOD TRUSS WITH METAL WEB

Web can be removed to allow for passage of pipes, ducts and wiring.

PLYWOOD WEB

WOOD TRUSS WITH WOOD WEB

KNOCKOUTS FOR WIRING

SOLID WOOD OR COMPOSITE WOOD FLANGE

WOOD "I" JOIST

Advantages of floor truss systems:
Greater strength than same size lumber; therefore, longer spans.
Better quality control of materials.
Easier installation of mechanical, plumbing and electrical systems.

Disadvantages of floor truss systems:
Less available.
More expensive for some applications.
Less flexible for field changes.

FLOOR TRUSS SYSTEMS

heavy exterior sheathing that adds vertical support to the house. The stud wall carries the vertical load of the house resting on top of the foundation walls.

Ask the builder to describe the entire wall system from the exterior through the interior with product names and benefits. The Wall System Profile, Exhibits 10.6 and 10.7, can be found on pages 138-140.

Exterior Finish

The exterior of a home makes an initial statement to every visitor. That statement might be any of the following:

- Looks like all the other houses

- Quality

- Ordinary—nothing special

- Prestigious

- Traditional Character

- Completely Charming

- Contemporary Pacesetter

- Comfortable

- Secure

. . . and the list goes on—reactions formulated just by seeing the exterior of the home—based on a combination of factors including design, roof lines and roof finish, exterior coverings, doors, windows and details such as the home—based on a combination of factors including design, roof lines and roof finish, exterior coverings, doors, windows and details such as mouldings, porch railings, lights and fireplace treatments. The questions in this section of the profile give you an opportunity to determine exactly what type of curb appeal these homes will have based on exterior finishes including driveway, sidewalks, patios and porches.

Exhibit 10.9 on page 143 will help you identify various door types. Windows are illustrated in Exhibit 10.10 on page 144.

Exhibit 10.6   Wall System Profile

1.   Exterior material:

NOTE: Types of material: brick, wood, alumi-num, vinyl, stone masonry, quoins, woodsiding including bevel, drop, shiplay, board and batten

2.   Exterior sheathing: the objective is to prevent entrance or penetration of moisture and weather; to prevent damaging decay, corrosion and insects and to provide reassurance, durability and economy of maintenance.

NOTE: Thickness and insulating factor

3.   Stud wall and bracing:

NOTE:
- 16" or 24" on center
- VA corner bracing straps or plywood sheathing on corners
- Size of studs

4.   Insulation:

NOTE:
- R-Value
- Blown or batten
- Is the insulation more than the local building code requires?

5.   Interior sheathing:

NOTE:
- Drywall or sheetrock
- Ceramic tile
- Panelling
- Stone
- Brick
- Plaster

NOTE: The purpose of interior sheathing is to provide a suitable base for decoration and to offer a waterproof surface that is durable and offers economy.

6.   Interior finishing, etc.:

NOTE: Paint, wallpaper, wood paneling, etc. Be specific with textures and types of up-grade features of the interior walls such as special mouldings. Remember the interior finish reflects the charm and character of the home; it is the emotional trigger in the showing of a new home!

7.   Other:

Refer to Exhibit 10.7 for a graphic depiction of stud walls with door and window openings featuring detailed labeling and the cross section of a wall from exterior finish to interior finish.

Exhibit 10.7   Wall Systems

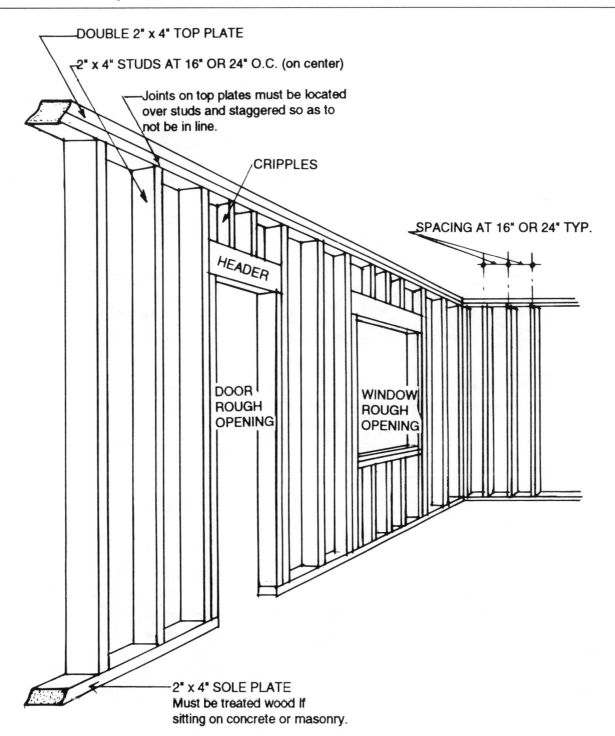

DOUBLE 2" x 4" TOP PLATE

2" x 4" STUDS AT 16" OR 24" O.C. (on center)

Joints on top plates must be located over studs and staggered so as to not be in line.

CRIPPLES

SPACING AT 16" OR 24" TYP.

HEADER

DOOR ROUGH OPENING

WINDOW ROUGH OPENING

2" x 4" SOLE PLATE
Must be treated wood if sitting on concrete or masonry.

STUD WALL

Exhibit 10.7 (cont'd)   Wall Systems

ROOF/CEILING

Studs at 12", 16", or 24" o.c.

WALL FINISH

JOISTS

BAND

STUDS
16" OR 24" o.c.

DOUBLE TOP PLATES

SECOND FLOOR SECTION

SHEATHING
1/8" to 1" or more plywood sheathing
or diagonal braces at corners.

WALL FRAMING

INSULATION

LAP SIDING

BUILDER'S FELT

SHEATHING

SILL PLATE ON
SILL SEALER

ANCHOR BOLTS
SET INTO
FOUNDATION WALL

SOLE PLATE

JOIST

TERMITE SHIELD

FOUNDATION WALL

FIRST FLOOR SECTION

WALL DETAILS

Interior Finish

When home shopping, the consumer dream-builds more in the interior of the home than anywhere else. Warm interiors reflecting distinctive styles, features and finishes provide emotional responses as consumers either feel the interior reminds them of previous homes or home features they've had, enjoyed or admired in another home or projects them into a future time and place where they've already envisioned themselves.

Question your builder carefully at this point to clarify three facts:

1. Is the builder finishing the interior so that it is compatible with the sales price of the home?

2. Are the items selected for the interior finish such as lights, cabinets, wall and floor coverings reflective of the character and quality of the design of the home? (If a builder is being squeezed financially at the end of building a home, some of the finish items are frequently skimped. This can be a fatal flaw—so listen carefully to these answers.)

3. Does the interior finish suit the proposed consumers? Example: If the product is a condominium community for active seniors and the interior is scheduled to be completed in a contemporary black and white color scheme throughout with passionate pink as the highlight color in baths, kitchen tiles and carpet borders in formal areas, there may be a problem. The interior finish package must conform to the historically established preferences of the targeted buyer groups understanding that those preferences can be enhanced through current trends in colors, use of textures and reflective surfaces.

Use these questions to enhance your knowledge of the builder's plans for the interiors of the homes and then determine if there is any flexibility on the part of the builder to make the changes you feel are necessary.

Soundproofing

The single largest complaint multi-family home purchasers have is noise. They hear washers draining, toilets flushing, people walking, stereos, TVs or company. These are serious concerns for you since you have built your career on providing families pride of ownership and personal peace and joy. These positive attributes hit the wall when the consumer experiences sudden interruptions caused by a neighbor's noise.

Exhibit 10.8   Exterior Finish Profile

List and describe the materials you will use to
finish the exterior of the homes in this community.

1. Exterior coverings:
   a. Type of material: NOTE: ■ Brick, wood, aluminum, vinyl,
                                                          stone, etc.
                                                        ■ If wood, will it be painted or stained?
                                                        ■ Will the purchaser choose color?
                                                        ■ If aluminum, does it have a smooth
                                                          woodgrain surface?
   b. Name Brands: NOTE: ■ Insulating factor
   c. List any special features of this type   ■ Maintenance free
      of covering: ■ Warranty or guarantee
                                                        ■ Upgrade features
   d. Other:
2. Doors and Windows: NOTE: Peachtree, Pella, Andersen?
   a. Name Brand: NOTE: If insulated, how are they insulated and
   b. Insulated or Non-Insulated: is there an insulating rating? If so, what
                                                        is it?
   c. Storm: NOTE: Stationary, removable glass and/or
   d. List any special features of this type   screen?
      of window.   NOTE: Frame: Is it aluminum or wood? Window:
                                                        Insulated frame? Vinyl clad frame?
3. Shutters: NOTE: Wood, aluminum, vinyl, etc.
   a. Type of material: NOTE: Custom-made or manufactured?
   b. Method of construction: NOTE: Permanently mounted with nails or
   c. Method of attachment: screws or mounted on shutter dogs
                                                        allowing the shutter to open and close.
   d. Size:
4. Trim Mouldings: NOTE: Wood or other—if wood what type; e.g.,
   a. Type of material: oak, pine, fur, etc.
   b. Size: NOTE: 1/2", 3/4", multi-layered, etc.
   c. Other: NOTE: Details

Patios and Decks
1. Are patios and decks standard or optional
   for this community? If standard, describe: NOTE: ■ Treated lumber
   a. Size: ■ Type of railing or banister
   b. Special features: ■ How many sets of steps/stairs
                                                        ■ Built-in seating
                                                        ■ Weight load

Driveway System
1. Describe the driveway system you will use   NOTE: ■ Paved
   in this community.   ■ Asphalt, concrete or brick
                                                        ■ Gravel
                                                        ■ Natural
                                                        ■ Aggregate

Yard
1. Describe, in detail, how you will complete   NOTE: Finished or rough
   each of the following: NOTE: ■ Sloped for proper drainage
   a. Grading: ■ Any underground drainage system
   b. Drainage:
   c. Landscaping: NOTE: Type of grass. Sprinkler systems
      1. Lawns   NOTE: More than mortgage requires?
      2. Shrubs and flowering plants
         (Types, number installed)   NOTE: Concrete, brick, wood, slate,
   d. Walkways: aggregate, lighted?

Exhibit 10.9   Door Types

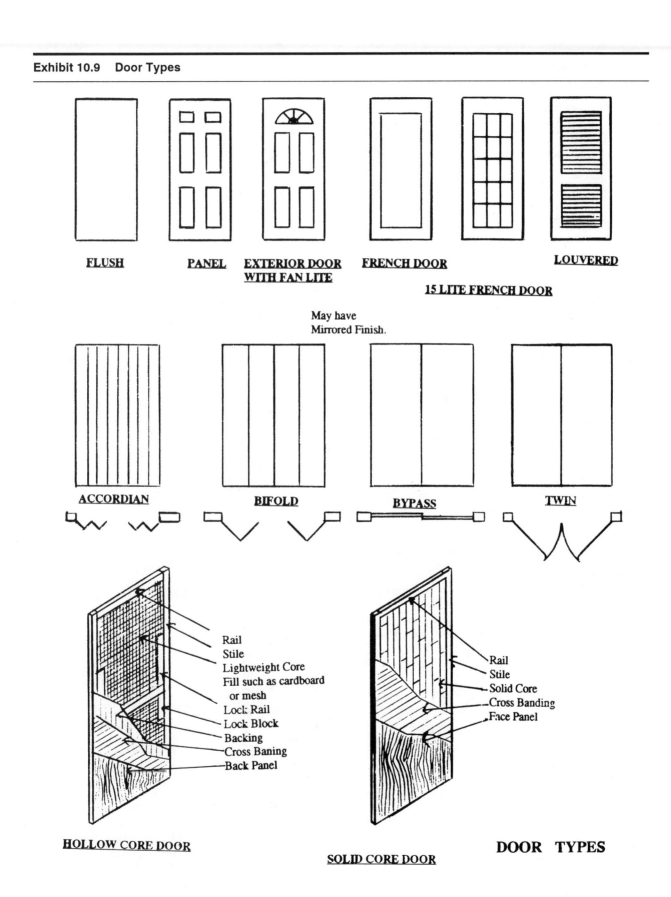

FLUSH   PANEL   EXTERIOR DOOR WITH FAN LITE   FRENCH DOOR   15 LITE FRENCH DOOR   LOUVERED

May have
Mirrored Finish.

ACCORDIAN   BIFOLD   BYPASS   TWIN

HOLLOW CORE DOOR
- Rail
- Stile
- Lightweight Core
- Fill such as cardboard or mesh
- Lock Rail
- Lock Block
- Backing
- Cross Baning
- Back Panel

SOLID CORE DOOR
- Rail
- Stile
- Solid Core
- Cross Banding
- Face Panel

DOOR TYPES

Exhibit 10.10 Windows

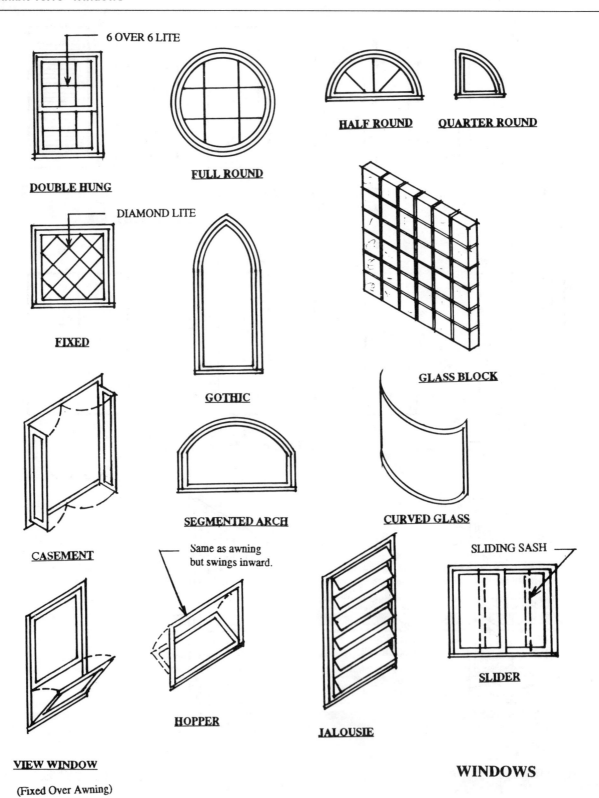

Exhibit 10.11 Interior Finish Profile

1. Floor Coverings:
   a. Foyer:
   b. Living areas:
   c. Kitchen:
   d. Baths:
   e. Bedrooms:
   f. If options are available such as upgrades, please quote the additional cost per room per house plan.

   NOTE: Include name brands, grade such as FHA approved *standard* carpet, and comfort and convenience features of each floor covering identified.

2. Walls
   a. Type of materials:
   b. Type of finish:
   c. If optional wall coverings are available, such as wallpaper, please quote the additional cost per room per house plan.

   NOTE: Drywall (sheetrock), paneling, etc.
   NOTE: Paint, wallpaper, etc.

3. Ceilings:
   a. Type of material:
   b. Type of finish:

   NOTE: Drywall (sheetrock)
   NOTE: Smooth or sprayed

4. Mouldings:
   a. Please list the type of material and the size for each of the following:
      1. Crown:
      2. Base:
      3. Chair Rail:
      4. Door:
      5. Window:
      6. Other:

   NOTE:
   - The material is usually wood.
   - The size of the moldings will vary. One determining factor of size is typically the price range of the house.

   NOTE: For example:
   - 3 1/4" colonial casing
   - 4 1/2" base
   - 2 member chair rail
   - 4 1/4" mullion with 3" chair rail
   - 2 member crown (Refer to Exhibit 10.6: Mouldings.)

5. Doors:
   a. Brand name:
   b. Solid or hollow-core:
   c. Hardware:

   NOTE: Smooth surface six panels
   NOTE:
   - Standard or upgrade, e.g., as an upgrade
   - With or without locks for interior doors
   - With or without glass transoms above the doors

6. Kitchen Cabinets:
   a. Single or double track drawers:
   b. What type of hardware do you use on the cabinets?
   c. Do you finish the back panel of the cabinets?

   NOTE: Metal or plastic tracks and rollers
   NOTE:
   - Metal, porcelain, etc.
   - If no, what closing is used?

   NOTE: Is there a back panel on the cabinets? If not, the back will be the wall and over time, as the visible portion of the wall is repainted, the portion of the wall under the cabinet will begin to "age."

Exhibit 10.11 (cont'd)   Interior Finish Profile

d.   Describe the type of countertops you use in your kitchens.

e.   Are cabinets custom or manufacturered?

- Pickled stain
- Traditional wood stains
- Reflective, polished surfaces such as gold, silver, pewter
- Glass doors available?

7.   Bath cabinets and vanities:

NOTE: See 6) a) above.

a.   Single or double track drawers:

NOTE: See 6) a) above.

b.   What type of hardware do you use on the cabinets?

NOTE: See 6) a) above.

c.   How do you finish the back of your cabinets?

d.   Describe how you finish the back countertops.

NOTE: Standard or upgrade, e.g., porcelain, enamel

e.   Do you use single or dual faucets?

NOTE: Where are they mounted? e.g. center or side of vanity, bevelled edge, vanity top to ceiling

f.   Describe the mirrors you use with your vanities.

NOTE: If wall mounted, how many fixtures are there and where are they mounted?

g.   Is your bath lighting mounted in the ceiling or the wall or both?

8.   Light fixtures:

a.   Describe, including brand names, the standard light fixtures you will use in the:

NOTE: Ceiling light or wall receptacle with wall switch operation or both?

1.   Living areas:

2.   Kitchen:

NOTE:
- Ceiling
- Over the range
- Over the sink
- Other

3.   Baths:

NOTE:
- Ceiling
- Wall mounted by mirrors
- Is there a light/fan combination?
- Over the bath or shower stall

4.   Bedrooms:

NOTE: Ceiling or wall switch operated or both?

5.   Closets and utility room(s):

NOTE: Look for a special feature.

6.   Front entrance:

NOTE: Wall mounted next to door

7.   Side and rear entrances:

NOTE: How many and the placement

8.   Spot, floor or area lights:

Exhibit 10.12 Mouldings

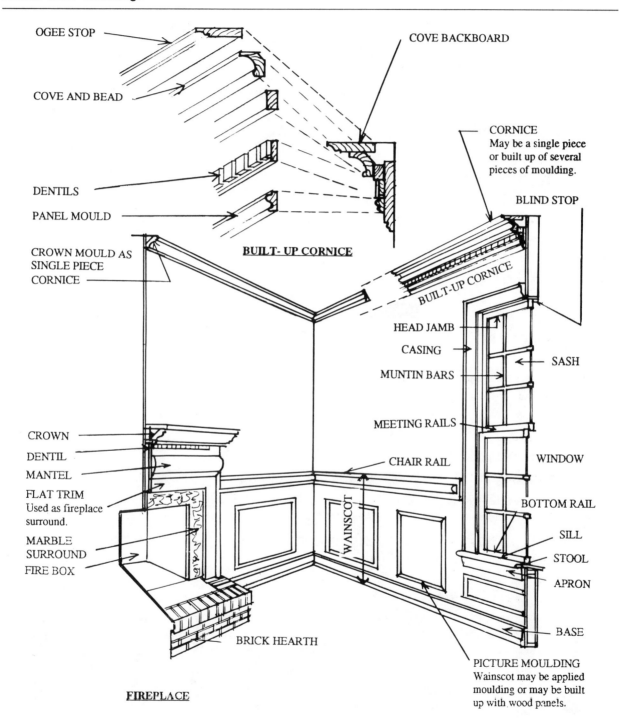

OGEE STOP

COVE AND BEAD

DENTILS

PANEL MOULD

COVE BACKBOARD

CORNICE
May be a single piece
or built up of several
pieces of moulding.

BLIND STOP

BUILT-UP CORNICE

CROWN MOULD AS
SINGLE PIECE
CORNICE

BUILT-UP CORNICE

HEAD JAMB

CASING

MUNTIN BARS

SASH

MEETING RAILS

CROWN

DENTIL

MANTEL

CHAIR RAIL

WINDOW

FLAT TRIM
Used as fireplace
surround.

WAINSCOT

BOTTOM RAIL

MARBLE
SURROUND
FIRE BOX

SILL

STOOL

APRON

BASE

BRICK HEARTH

PICTURE MOULDING
Wainscot may be applied
moulding or may be built
up with wood panels.

FIREPLACE

MOULDING APPLICATIONS

Exhibit 10.12 (cont'd)   Mouldings

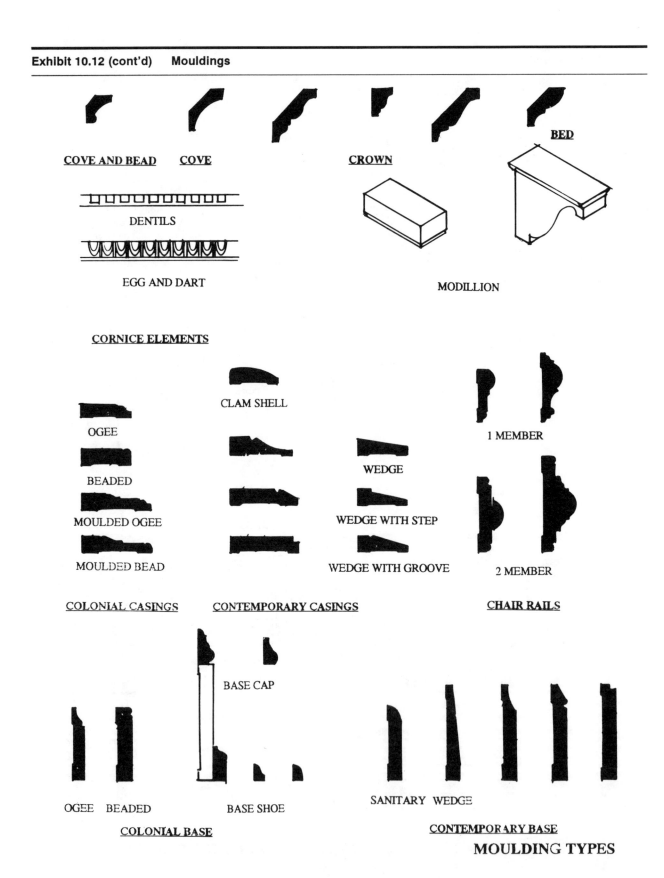

COVE AND BEAD   COVE

CROWN

BED

DENTILS

EGG AND DART

MODILLION

CORNICE ELEMENTS

OGEE

CLAM SHELL

BEADED

MOULDED OGEE

WEDGE

MOULDED BEAD

WEDGE WITH STEP

WEDGE WITH GROOVE

1 MEMBER

2 MEMBER

COLONIAL CASINGS   CONTEMPORARY CASINGS   CHAIR RAILS

BASE CAP

OGEE   BEADED   BASE SHOE   SANITARY WEDGE

COLONIAL BASE   CONTEMPORARY BASE

MOULDING TYPES

Exhibit 10.12 (cont'd)   Mouldings

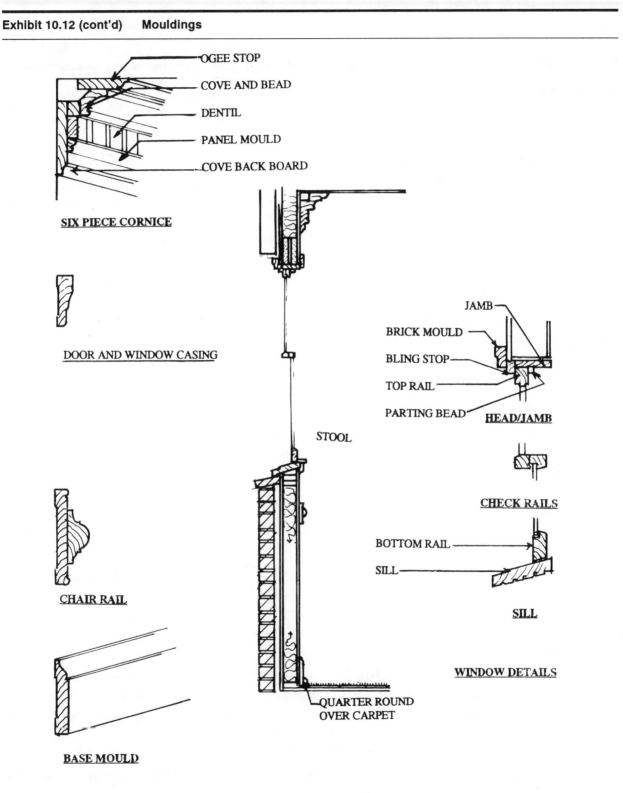

OGEE STOP

COVE AND BEAD

DENTIL

PANEL MOULD

COVE BACK BOARD

SIX PIECE CORNICE

DOOR AND WINDOW CASING

JAMB

BRICK MOULD

BLING STOP

TOP RAIL

PARTING BEAD

HEAD/JAMB

CHECK RAILS

STOOL

BOTTOM RAIL

SILL

SILL

CHAIR RAIL

WINDOW DETAILS

QUARTER ROUND
OVER CARPET

BASE MOULD

MOULDINGS

Exhibit 10.13 Plumbing Systems

Today's consumers are interested in long-term, functional reliability from their plumbing systems while being surrounded by convenience and luxury in their baths and kitchens. They are primarily interested in the number of baths, types of appliances in each and the brand names being used. It is important for the builder to cover the following primary points:

1. Describe the plumbing system you will use, including types of drain pipes, fixtures, etc., and be sure to list brand names.
    a. Kitchen:
    b. Baths:
    c. Laundry:
    d. Exterior:
    e. Other:

NOTE:
- Look for upscale features especially in the kitchen and baths.
- Look for anything "beyond code" in your local market.
- Examples:
    - 2 1/2" to 3" PVC or plastic waste lines
    - 1/2" copper water supply lines
    - Cast iron drain pipes designed to eliminate waste water sounds
    - Kohler, Delta, Moen etc. fixtures
    - Washerless (or not)
    - If the community includes multi-family dwellings, it is important to ask how the drainpipes are insulated for soundproofing.
    - Ask about the type of water and sewer systems whether private as in well and septic or public.

The nation's builders, building suppliers and architects are aggressively attacking the noise problem. Builders have several *soundproofing* options. They can:

- Use insulated exterior doors and windows.

- Increase all insulation in exterior walls, ceilings overhead and in the floor systems.

- Add gypcrete, a concrete product that is poured on top of sub flooring in 1/2" application. When dried, the surface is ready for carpet padding and carpeting. It significantly reduces noise from one floor to the next.

- Increase carpet padding and carpet thickness throughout the house.

- Use cast iron drainpipes throughout and pack insulation around them to muffle sound.

- Use double thicknesses of common walls with double insulation.

- If concrete block common walls are used, insulate the center of the block with foam or blown insulation.

- Insulate all *interior* walls to further soundproof the interior.

- Use "quiet" feature dishwashers and appliances.

- Place cable TV hook up outlets on exterior walls to reduce noise.

The final step that can be taken to control noise in multi-family homes is to have the restrictive covenants stipulate moderate noise levels as acceptable when using TVs, stereos and radios. Certainly, a tremendous sales plus in this industry is the ability to offer a "quiet home" to your harried consumers.

Insulation

As you interview the builder on this point, ask for identification of every possible energy saving feature of the home including discounts available to the consumers. Today's consumer is extremely sensitive to conservation from both an ecological and cost effective perspective. It becomes your responsibility to urge your builders to offer more insulation than is required by local building codes. Note the standard insulation tables that apply nationally. Be very specific in your builder discussion at this point. It can mean future sales for you.

The purpose of insulation is to control moisture, heat, sound, economy and soundproofing for the energy efficient home. Typically, you are asked to explain the "R" factors of insulation. "R" simply means the degree of resistance to heat or cold that insulation offers—the higher the "R"-value, the more insulated the home. Insulation also has a vapor barrier designed to face the inside of the home to prevent the transfer of outside moisture to the inside of your home.

The Insulation Profile can be found in Exhibit 10.14 on page 153.

Electrical Features and Systems

The lighting and electrical features of a home set the stage for mood, comfort and convenience, and consumers are very demanding in these areas. Security systems, intercoms, remote control garage door systems, built-in humidifiers, and luxurious lighting are inherent expectations on the part of upper income purchasers. Fifteen years ago, many of these systems were reserved for only the most elite properties. Today, they are standard fare in various areas of the country, such as urban locations, the west coast and in upper middle income properties everywhere.

It is important to your sales success that you clearly define what is standard for the builder in this regard and what represents an upgrade to the consumer. Local building codes strictly identify the type of wiring to be used throughout the home, the maximum distance between wall receptacles (outlets) beginning six feet from every door opening and the specific number of lights to be used per square foot of space. Local building codes also identify the number of exterior lights to be used and the restrictive covenants of many neighborhoods stipulate exactly what types of lights are required and where—such as lampposts at the end of every front sidewalk. Lighted doorbells are also identified as standard.

Note that the questions on the profile in Exhibit 10.16 on page 155 are designed to specifically identify what the builder offers as standard in order to provide you with sales advantages.

Roof Systems

Home value has long been partially determined by roof design. Today both the design and the roof covering are primary ingredients to home value. Historically, only upgrade sheathings such as slate, clay tiles, cedar shakes or shingles added significant values to home prices. Today, the sky is the limit when considering all of the roof coverings available—from a simple poured roof to a standard fiberglass shingle, to a textured shingle to an architectural grade shingle. Each of these progressively improved roof coverings offers improved value.

You must be well versed in pointing out the pluses of the roof coverings and understand the hidden value inherent in the roof framing. The profile in Exhibit 10.17 on pages 156-157 specifically questions the type of support system—truss or rafter and joist, as well as type and quality of sheathing. Know this area of the home thoroughly to capture the very highest degree of buyer support for your product.

Exhibit 10.14 Insulation Profile

---

1. Describe the insulation you use, giving R-factors   NOTE: ■   Blown or batten?

    and benefits to the buyer.   ■   Do you seal around doors,

                                                                        windows and wire holes?

    a.   Ceiling/Roof: ■   If yes, what material do you seal

    b.   Walls: with?

    c.   Floors: ■   Do you insulate beyond the levels

                                                                        required by the local building

                                                                        codes?

2. Will your type of insulation and method of   NOTE: If yes, how much of a discount?

    installation qualify for the local power company's

    energy discount?

3. What type of insulation material do you use?

    a.   Fiber Insulation Board

    b.   Soft Wood Fiber (this is used in extremely

          cold climates)

    c.   Vermiculite

    d.   Reflective Types/Aluminum

    e.   Styrofoam

    f.   Mineral Wool

    g.   Vegetable Fiber

Gutters and Downspouts

Gutters and downspouts preserve landscaping and finish grading by protecting them from the soil erosion that results from torrents of rainwater cascading from the roof. Gutters and downspouts allow the orderly collection and distribution of rainwater, diverting it from entrances to the property, foundation walls and landscaping. Gutters are particularly desirable when overhangs are small.

■ Are gutters and downspouts standard or optional?

■ If optional, what is the price to install gutters and downspouts?

■ Are splash blocks provided under all downspouts as standard?

Exhibit 10.15 Heating and Cooling Systems Profile

Heating and cooling systems are a second major concern of today's consumer. Desirable systems offer a comfortable, climate-controlled environment while at the same time featuring optimum efficiency and energy savings. Most areas offer primary fuels that are most cost effective and comfortable for that particular geographical locale, such as natural gas in the Midwest. Builders who supply houses that utilize this more cost effective fuel source have deleted one area of future purchaser objections. This section is designed to highlight only the most fundamental aspects of the heating and cooling systems that would be of concern to your purchasers. You are encouraged to master this information and use it in your presentation.

Describe in detail the heating/cooling system you will use in this community.

1.   Type of system:

NOTE: Gas, L.P. Oil, Electricity, Coal, Wood and solar.

NOTE:
■   Convection—traveling through the vents
■   Radiant—passive delivery system in which heat radiates from a stationary heat source such as radiators and ceiling or baseboard electric heat
■   Conduction—conducts heated water to a heat source such as a radiator

2.   Size of system:
3.   Name brand:

NOTE: Today's consumer recognizes name brands from the media. Offer manufacturer brochures that answer questions about the system for the consumer.

4.   What are the typical monthly energy costs for this system in your homes?
   a.   3 bedroom homes:
   b.   4 bedroom homes:
   c.   Larger, executive style homes:
   d.   Do you have a copy of the local power company's computer printout regarding this system's estimated energy costs? If no, call the power company and get one.

NOTE: If yes, ask for a copy.

5.   What is the advantage of this system?

NOTE: Typical answers would be:
■   Lower energy cost
■   Lower maintenance

6.   Do you use split system in multi-level or bi-level homes? If yes, please describe the system. What size systems do you use in your homes?

NOTE: The type of system is governed by the size and layout of the home. To determine size, the following works well. Multiply the square footage of the house x 60 = BTU's (British Thermal Units of Energy) needed to heat the home with gas or oil.

7.   What type of duct system do you use in you homes?
   a.   Type:
   b.   Advantage:
   c.   Do you wrap your ducts with insulation? Are floor registers or ceiling registers placed under or above windows?

NOTE:
■   Metal ducts are wrapped with insulation to assure greater climate control of the air. These ducts can be mounted in the attic area or under the floor system in the crawl space or basement. They are sometimes mounted on ceilings and concealed behind sheetrock.
■   Flex duct offers easy installation to any area of the home. It is self-insulated. The advantage here is ease of installation.

Exhibit 10.16 Electrical System Profile

---

1. Describe, other than by code, the type of wiring you use.

    NOTE: ■ Ask for the size of wiring e.g., 10-2, 12-2, etc.
    ■ Copper or aluminum

2. Describe, other than by code, your criteria for placement of wall receptacles. Be specific in describing distances from wall openings, etc.

    NOTE: The most common answer to this question is "by code." Ask the Builder to be specific, e.g., every 6' of wall space.

3. List all items for which wiring is standard in every home you build. For example, kitchen range.

    NOTE: ■ Range
    ■ Refrigerator
    ■ Trash Compactor
    ■ Telephone Jacks
    ■ Doorbell or Chimes
    ■ Security System
    ■ Range Hood
    ■ Disposal
    ■ Washer/Dryer
    ■ Cable TV
    ■ Microwave

    a.
    b.
    c.
    d.
    e.
    f.
    g.
    h.
    i.
    j.
    k.

4. What is your standard light fixture allowance?

    NOTE: There are four typical answers to this question:
    1. None
    2. A flat dollar amount, e.g. $500.
    3. A flat dollar amount with the option of shopping at a local lighting supplier with builder discount
    4. A percentage of the sales price with the builder discount to be used at a local supplier (This option is typically reserved for custom homes, either single family or multi-family.) Builder Discount at most lighting centers is 1/2 of the retail price; thus a $500 light would be sold with a discount of $250.

5. Is wiring for ceiling fans standard or optional?
    a.
    b. If optional, have the builder quote an additional fee per house plan per feature, e.g., per fan, per spotlight, etc.

6. Is wiring for exterior spotlights standard or optional?
    a.

    NOTE: See the answer under 2. above

    b. If optional, what is the additional fee?

Exhibit 10.17   Roof Systems Profile

What type of roof system will you use in this community?

1. Type of Roof System:
   a. Rafter which is stick build onsite, solid wood (This system is the universally recognized tried and proven application.)
   b. Truss which is a manufactured product produced in a factory and delivered to the site ready for installation.

NOTE:
- Rafter and joist or truss?
- If rafter and joist, ask the size of each, e.g., 2" by 6", 2" by 8", etc.

2. What type of roof decking are you using?

NOTE:
- Type of material: 1/2" plywood is standard applied with roof clips to allow for expansion and contraction. If an extremely heavy roof is being installed, the roof decking might be a series of horizontal beams to which tiles are attached.

3. Type of Sheathing:

NOTE: Felt—typically 15 lb. asphalt. Saturated felt is used on top of the roof sheathing to retard moisture penetration. Felt underlay is available in heavier weights for use in colder weather.

4. Type and Weight of Underlayment:

5. Type of Shingles:

NOTE:
- Asphalt with reflecting granulars
- Wood
- Tile
- Slate
- Fiberglass (20 yr. life)
- Textured Fiberglass (25 yr. life)
- Architectural Grade Fiberglass (30 yr. life)
- Cedar Shakes
- Cedar Shingles
- Masonite Shingles (designed to look like slate with a 40-yr. life)

6. Type of Ventilation System:
   a. Roof:

NOTE:
- Ridge vent is at the peak of the roof where rafters meet. Ridge vent would be located on the peak of the roof and can work only along the eaves of the home.
- The passive gable is located in the gable ends of the house and relies on natural air patterns to cool the attic area.
- Power vents, usually in the gable ends of the home, have power driven exhaust fans and automatic timers.

Exhibit 10.17 (cont'd)   Roof Systems Profile

b.   Overhand:

NOTE: Soffit venting can be mounted in the overhand (eave) as vents placed periodically or continuous soffit vents to run the full length of all eaves to work in conjunction with a ridge vent. This promotes constant circle air exchange from outside air pulled up through the soffit vent through the attic and out the ridge vent.

7.   Describe the advantages of this roof system:

NOTE:
- Ridge vent: No cost to operate
- Passive Gable: No cost to operate, but lacks the efficiency of a ridge vent system
- Power Gables: Optimum personal control of attic air exchange through automatic timer

Refer to the illustrations in Exhibit 10.18 for self-instruction. They are also useful when explaining one of the roof systems to buyers.

Exhibit 10.18   Roof Systems

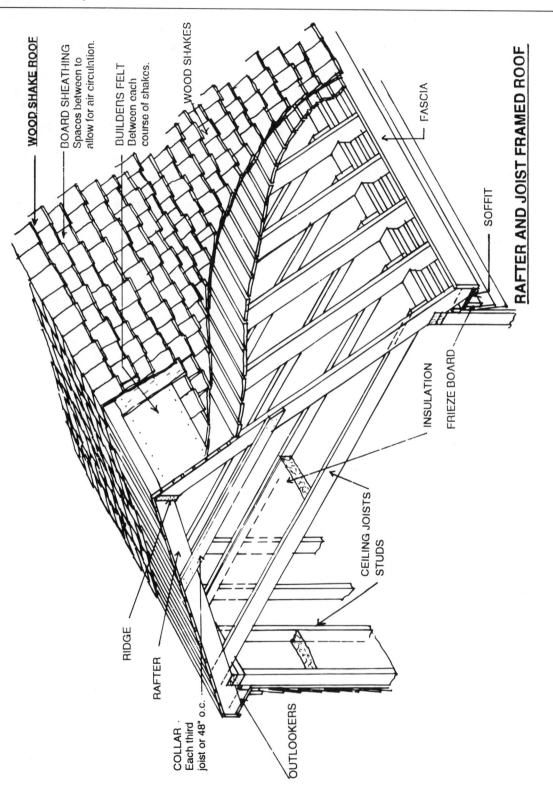

Exhibit 10.18 (cont'd)   Roof Systems

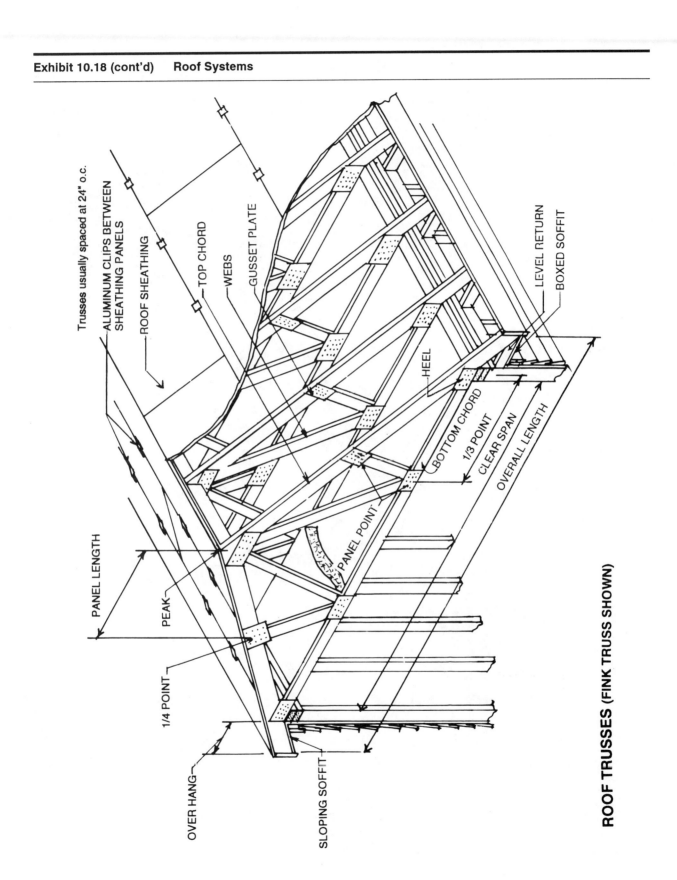

ROOF TRUSSES (FINK TRUSS SHOWN)

Exhibit 10.18 (cont'd)   Roof Systems

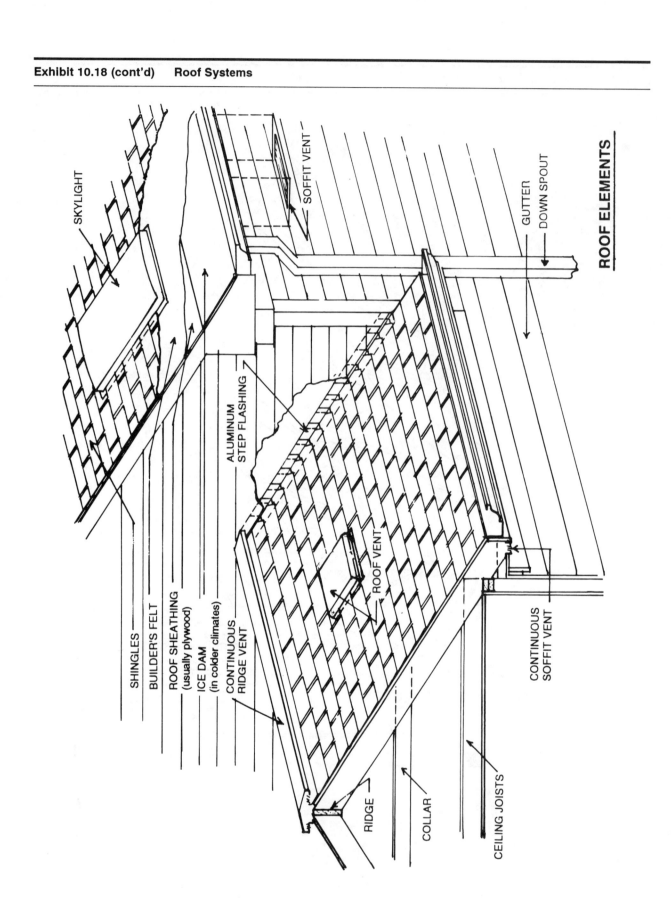

ROOF ELEMENTS

SKYLIGHT

SOFFIT VENT

GUTTER

DOWN SPOUT

SHINGLES

BUILDER'S FELT

ROOF SHEATHING
(usually plywood)

ICE DAM
(in colder climates)

CONTINUOUS
RIDGE VENT

ALUMINUM
STEP FLASHING

ROOF VENT

CONTINUOUS
SOFFIT VENT

RIDGE

COLLAR

CEILING JOISTS

Exhibit 10.18 (cont'd)   Roof Systems

FLAT

GABLE

DOUBLE SHED
(Saw Tooth)

HIP

GAMBREL

DUTCH HIP

MANSARD

SALT BOX

ROOF TYPES

The Knowledgeable Interviewer

As you read the profiles, were you able to create an image of yourself in a builder's office with your questions being answered? Were you able to picture yourself walking out of the builder's office feeling like you knew as much as possible about the community? You should—that's one of the primary purposes of the profile.

As discussed earlier, you must be involved in asking questions and carefully listening to the builder's answers in order to personally gain maximum benefit from the profile. If the builder gives an answer that either seems incomplete or you do not understand, ask for an explanation. (This occurs with some builders when the most obvious answer is "by code.") Don't be overbearing with your questions, but take advantage of every opportunity to impress.

To broaden your language base and enhance your understanding of the components of a new home, read and study the *Glossary of Building Terms* below. Its most useful application involves a visit to a new home site under construction with products in various stages of completion. Try to locate and identify every item defined in the glossary. This is even more fun and enlightening if you can have the builder or construction superintendent assist you in the exercise. Usually they are delighted to assist since they know that the more you know about their product, the more prospects you can convert to purchasers.

Glossary of Building Terms

acoustical tile   A special tile for walls and ceilings made of mineral, wood, vegetable fibers, cork, or metal, used to control sound volume, while providing cover.

air duct   Pipes that carry warm and cold air to rooms and back to the furnace or air conditioning systems.

ampere   The rate of flow of electricity through electric wires.

apron   A paved area such as the juncture of a driveway with the street or with a garage entrance.

backfill   The gravel or earth replaced in the space around a building wall after foundations are in place.

balusters   Upright supports of a balustrade rail.

balustrade   Row of balusters topped by rail edging, balcony or staircase.

baseboard   A board along floor against walls and partitions to hide gaps.

batt   Insulation in the form of a blanket.

batten   Small thin strips covering joints between wider boards on exterior building surfaces.

beam   A principal horizontal wood or steel member of a building.

bearing wall   A wall that supports the floor or roof of a building.

bib or bibcock   A water faucet to which a hose may be attached, also called a hose bib or sill cock.

bleeding   Resin/gum seeping from lumber; drawing air from water pipes.

brace   A piece of wood or other material used to form a triangle and stiffen part of a structure.

braced framing   A construction technique using posts and crossbracing for greater rigidity.

brick veneer   Brick used as the outer surface of a framed wall.

bridging   Diagonally wood or metal pieces between floor joists.

building paper   Heavy paper used in walls or roofs to dampproof.

build-up roof   A roofing material applied in sealed, waterproof layers, where there is only a slight slope to the roof.

butt joint   Joining point of two pieces of wood or molding.

bx cable   Electricity cable wrapped in rubber with flexible steel covering.

cantilever   A projecting beam or joist, not supported at one end, used to support an extension of a structure.

carriage   The member which supports the steps or treads of a stair.

casement   A window sash that opens on hinges at the vertical edge.

casing   Door and window framing.

cavity wall   A hollow wall formed by firmly linked masonry walls, providing an insulating air space between.

chair rail   Wooden molding on wall around room at chair back level.

chamfered edge   Molding with pared-off corners.

chase   Groove in wall or through floor to accommodate pipes or ducts.

chimney breast   The horizontal projection—usually inside a building—of a chimney from the wall in which it is built.

chimney cap   Concrete capping around the top of chimney bricks and around the floors to protect the masonry from the elements.

circuit breaker   A safety device that opens (breaks) an electric circuit automatically when it becomes overloaded.

cistern   A tank that catches and stores rainwater.

clapboard   A long thin board, thicker on one edge, overlapped and nailed on for exterior siding.

collar beam   A horizontal beam fastened above the lower ends of rafters to add rigidity.

coping   Tile or brick used to cap or cover the top of a masonry wall.

corbel   A horizontal projection from a wall, forming a ledge or supporting a structure above it.

corner bead   A strip of wood or metal for protecting the external corners of plastered walls.

cornice   A horizontal projection at the top of a wall or under the overhanging part of the roof.

course   Horizontal row of bricks, cinder blocks or other masonry materials.

cove lighting   Concealed light sources behind a cornice or horizontal recess that direct the light upon a reflecting ceiling.

crawl space   Shallow, unfinished space beneath first floor of a house that has no basement, used for visual inspection and access to pipes and ducts; also, shallow space in attic, immediately under roof.

cripples   Cut-off framing members above and below windows.

door buck   The rough frame of a door.

dormer   The projecting frame of a recess in a sloping roof.

double glazing   An insulating windowpane formed of two thicknesses of glass with a sealed air space between them.

double hung windows   Windows with an upper and lower sash, each supported by cords and weights.

downspout   Spout or pipe to carry rainwater down from roof or gutters.

downspout leader   A pipe for conducting rainwater from the roof to a cistern or to the ground by way of a downspout.

downspout strap   A piece of metal that secures the downspout to the eaves or wall of a building.

drip   The projecting part of a cornice that sheds rainwater.

dry wall   A wall surface of plasterboard or material other than plaster.

eaves   The extension of a roof beyond house walls.

efflorescence   White powder that forms on the surface of brick.

effluent   Treated sewage from a septic tank or sewage treatment plant.

fascia   A flat horizontal member of a cornice placed in a vertical position.

fill-type insulation   Loose insulating material that is applied by hand or mechanically blown into wall spaces.

flashing   Noncorrosive metal used around angles or junctions in roofs and exterior walls to prevent leaks.

floor joists   Framing pieces that rest on outer foundation walls and interior beams or girders.

flue   A passageway in a chimney for conveying smoke, gases or fumes to the outside air.

footing   Concrete base on which a foundation sits.

foundation   Lower parts of walls on which structure is built; foundation walls of masonry or concrete mainly below ground level.

framing   The rough lumber of a house—joists, studs, rafters and beams.

furring   Thin wood or metal applied to a wall to level the surface for lathing, boarding, or plastering, in order to create an insulating air space and dampproof the wall.

fuse   A short plug in an electric panel box which opens (breaks) an electrical circuit when it becomes overloaded.

gable   The triangular part of a wall under the inverted "V" of the roof line.

gambrel roof   Roof with two pitches, designed to provide more space on upper floors—steeper on its lower slope and flatter toward the ridge.

girder   A main member in a framed floor supporting the joists that carry the flooring boards; it carries the weight of a floor or partition.

glazing   Fitting glass into windows or doors.

grade line   Point at which the ground rests against the foundation wall.

green lumber   Lumber that has been inadequately dried and tends to warp or "bleed" resin.

grounds   Pieces of wood embedded in the plaster of walls to which skirtings are attached; also wood pieces used to stop the plaster work around doors and windows.

gusset   A brace or bracket used to strengthen a structure.

gutter   A channel at the eaves for conveying rainwater.

hardwood   The close-grained wood from broad leaved trees such as oak or maple.

headers   Double wood pieces supporting joists in a floor or double wood members placed on edge over windows and doors to transfer the roof and floor weight to the studs.

heel   The end of a rafter that rests on the wall plate.

hip roof   A roof that slants upward on three or four sides.

hip   The external angle formed by the juncture of two slopes of a roof.

jalousies   Windows or shutters with movable, horizontal slats angled to admit ventilation and keep out rain.

joist   A small rectangular sectional member arranged parallel from wall to wall in a building or resting on beams or girders that support a floor or the furring strips of a ceiling.

kiln-dried   An artificial method of drying lumber, superior to most lumber that is air-dried.

king-post   The middle post of a truss.

lag-screws or coach-screws   Large, heavy screws, used for great strength, as in heavy framing or when attaching ironwork to wood.

lally column A steel tube sometimes filled with concrete used to support girders or other floor beams.

lath A thin narrow strip of wood nailed to rafters, ceiling joists, wall studs, etc. to make a groundwork or key for slates, tiles, or plastering.

leaching bed Trench tiles carrying treated wastes from septic tanks.

ledger A piece of wood that is attached to a beam to support joists.

lintel Top piece over door or window that supports walls above opening.

load-bearing wall A strong wall capable of supporting weight.

louver An opening with horizontal slats to permit passage of air, excluding rain, sunlight and view.

masonry Walls built using brick, stone, tile or similar materials.

molding A strip of decorative material having a plain or curved narrow surface prepared for ornamental application; often used to hide gaps at wall junctures.

moisture barrier Treated paper or metal that retards or bars water vapor, used to keep moisture from passing into walls or floors.

mullion Slender framing that divides the lights or panes of windows.

newel The upright post or the upright formed by the inner or smaller ends of steps around which the steps of a circular staircase wind; in a straight flight staircase, the principal post at the foot or the secondary post at a landing.

nosing The rounded edge of a stair tread.

parging A rough coat of motor oil applied over a masonry wall as protection or finish; may also serve as a base for an asphaltic waterproofing compound below grade.

pilaster A projection or the foundation wall used to support a floor girder or stiffen the wall.

pitch The angle or slope of a roof.

plasterboard (See Dry Wall) Gypsum board, used instead of plaster.

plates Pieces of wood placed on wall surfaces as fastening devices—the bottom member of the wall is the sole plate and the top member is the rafter plate.

plenum Chamber that serves as a distribution area for heating or cooling systems, generally between a false ceiling and the actual ceiling.

pointing Treatment of joints in masonry accomplished by filling with mortar to improve appearance or protect against weather.

post-and-beam construction Wall construction in which beams are supported by heavy posts rather than many smaller studs.

prefabrication Construction of components such as walls, trusses or doors before delivery to the building site.

rabbet A groove cut in a board to receive another board.

radiant heat   Coils of electricity, hot water or steam pipes embedded in floors, ceilings, or walls to heat rooms.

rafter   One of a series of structural roof members spanning from an exterior wall to a center ridge beam or ridge board.

reinforced concrete   Concrete strengthened with wire or metal bars.

ridge pole   Thick longitudinal plank where roof's ridge rafters attach.

risers   The upright piece of a stair step, from tread to tread.

roof sheathing   Sheets, usually of plywood, nailed to top edges of trusses or rafters to tie roof together and support roofing material.

sandwich panel   A panel with plastic, paper or other material enclosed between two layers of a different material.

sash   The movable part of a window; the frame in which panes of glass are set in a window or door.

scotia   A concave molding.

scuttle hole   A small opening either to the attic, to the crawl space or the plumbing pipes.

seepage pit   A sewage disposal system composed of a septic tank and a connected cesspool.

septic tank   A sewage setting tank in which part of the sewage is converted into gas and sludge before the remaining waste is discharged by gravity into an underground leaching bed.

shakes   Hand-cut wood shingles.

sheathing   The first covering of boards or material on the outside wall or roof prior to installing the finished siding or roof covering.

shim   A thin tapered piece of wood used for leveling or tightening a stair or other building element.

shingles   Pieces of wood, asbestos or other material used as an overlapping outer covering on walls or roofs.

shiplap   Boards with overlapping rabbeted edges.

siding   Boards of special design nailed horizontally to vertical studs with or without intervening sheathing to form the exposed surface of outside walls of frame buildings.

sill plate   The lowest member of the house framing resting on top of the foundation wall; also called the mud sill.

skirting   Narrow boards around the margin of the floor; baseboards.

slab   Concrete floor placed directly on earth or a gravel base and usually about four inches thick.

sleeper   Strip of wood laid over concrete floor to which the finished wood floor is nailed or glued.

soffit   The visible underside of structural members such as staircases, cornices, beams, a roof overhead or eave.

softwood   Easily worked wood or wood from a cone-bearing tree.

soil stack   Vertical plumbing pipe for waste water.

stringer   A long, horizontal member that connects uprights in a frame or supports a floor or the like; one of the enclosed sides of a stair supporting the treads and risers.

studs   In wall framing, the vertical members to which horizontal pieces are nailed—spaced either 16 inches or 24 inches apart.

subfloor   Usually, plywood sheets that are nailed directly to the floor joists and receive the finish flooring.

sump   A pit in the basement in which water collects to be pumped out with a sump pump.

swale   A wide shallow depression in the ground that forms a channel for stormwater drainage.

tile   A wood member that binds a pair of principal rafters at the bottom.

tile field   Open-joint drain tiles laid to distribute septic tank effluent over an absorption area or to provide subsoil drainage in wet areas.

toenail   Driving nails at an angle into corners or other joints.

tongue-and-groove   Carpentry joint in which the jutting edge of one board fits into the grooved end of a similar board.

trap   A bend in a water pipe to hold water so gases will not escape from the plumbing system into the house.

trend   The horizontal part of a stair step.

truss   Combination of structural members usually in triangular units to form rigid framework for spanning between load-bearing walls.

valley   The depression at the meeting point of two roof slopes.

vapor barrier   Material such as paper, metal or paint that is used to prevent vapor from passing from rooms into the outside walls.

venetian window   A window with one large fixed central pane and smaller panes at each side.

vent pipe   A pipe that allows gas to escape from plumbing systems.

verge   Edge of tiles, slates or shingles, projecting over the gable of a roof.

wainscoting   The lower three or four feet of an interior wall when lined with paneling, tile or other material different from the rest of the wall.

wall sheathing   Sheets of plywood, gypsum board or other material nailed to the outside face of studs as a base for exterior siding.

weather stripping   Metal, wood, plastic or other material installed around door and window openings to prevent air infiltration.

weep hole   A small hole in a wall that permits water to drain off.

11

Marketing for Success

Simply defined, marketing is the development, coordination and implementation of a unified plan of action that results in the positive acceptance of your product, goods or services. A strong platform for sales activities, marketing has been defined as the sizzle that sells the steak, or the glitz and glamour that sell the diamonds, minks or Mercedes. It is also true that New Homes Marketing Programs set the stage for emotional appeals that condition sales results to be more profitable for the agent and the builder. This is accomplished through the use of merchandised models, sales presentation arenas, dramatic signage, entry graphics, brochures, major and minor events for both REALTOR® communities and the public, incentive campaigns and advertising.

Evaluation of the Site

In order to know what setting your stage requires, you must first evaluate and inspect your builder's site. Exhibit 11.1 on page 170 is an easy outline for the inspection, providing a base from which to develop a marketing program.

Exhibit 11.1   Site Evaluation Form

NAME OF COMMUNITY _____

DATE OF EVALUATION _____

    I.   COMMUNITY AREA

What is to the immediate left and right of the property?

_____

_____

What is immediately in front of and behind the property?

_____

_____

What is in the general vicinity of the property?

_____

_____

Comments _____

_____

_____

    II.   Offsite Signage—(banners, directional signs)

Was there any offsite signage? YES or NO

If yes, describe.

_____

_____

If there was no offsite signage where could signage be placed?

_____

_____

   III. Entry of Community

What impact did the entry sign create?

_____

_____

What was the entry sign made of?

_____

_____

_____

Exhibit 11.1 (cont'd)   Site Evaluation Form

Was the area around the sign landscaped?

_____

_____

_____

Was the sign lighted? YES or NO (street lamp next to it?)
Were there seasonal plantings? YES or NO (everything in bloom?)
Was the overall landscaping well maintained? YES or NO
Comments:

_____

_____

_____

IV.   Onsite Signage
Were directional signs present? YES or NO
Was there a sign on the model? YES or NO
Was a sign with hours of operation present? YES or NO
Was there a sign listing the marketing company's name? YES or NO
Comments:

_____

_____

_____

V.   Models and Merchandising
Was music playing? YES or NO
If yes, what type of music?

_____

Was there a pleasant fragrance in the models? YES or NO
If yes, what type of fragrance?

_____

_____

What type of greeting did you get from the agent?

_____

_____

Was the agent's desk area neat? YES or NO
Describe the agent's office area.

_____

_____

_____

Exhibit 11.1 (cont'd)   Site Evaluation Form

Were model signs present? YES or NO

Did model signs fit the theme of the community? YES or NO

What did the model signs look like?

_____

_____

How many models were at the community? _____

Please describe the merchandising (type of furniture for type of people there).

Model One _____

_____

Model Two _____

_____

Model Three _____

_____

Model Four _____

_____

VI.   Guest Registration and Collaterals

Were you given a brochure and price list? YES or NO

Did the brochure fit the community theme? YES or NO

Did the agent use a registration card? YES or NO

Any suggestions for collaterals?

_____

_____

VII. Suggestions for community

Community area information

_____

_____

Offsite signage

_____

_____

Exhibit 11.1 (cont'd)   Site Evaluation Form

Community entry

_____

_____

_____

Onsite signage

_____

_____

_____

Models and merchandising

_____

_____

_____

Guest registration and collaterals

_____

_____

_____

The Site Evaluation inspection affords you the foundation to use in developing marketing programs in any of the following areas :

- Signage
- Entry Graphics
- Landscaping and Street Furniture
- Models
- Sales Center
- Theme
- Name and Logo
- Brochures and Collaterals
- Displays
- Advertising and Marketing Plan of Action
    - Print

- Radio

- Television

- Direct Mail

- Video

- Outdoor/Billboards

- Events—Broker and Public

■ Public Relations

It would be wonderful if, after inspecting the site and deciding the areas in which you needed marketing direction, you could magically produce signage, brochures and media programs that would guarantee sales success. Marketing is a living, breathing activity that is constantly changing. Unfortunately, there is no instant marketing soup in which you put two parts of creativity mixed with two parts of financial backing with an end result of guaranteed sales success.

Certainly, marketing demands an analysis of the buyer as well as an analysis of area demographics and the competitor's strategies. With that research and the realization that the national economy, international peace and buyer attitudes will dictate changes in your marketing programs, it's time to develop your strategies.

This chapter is *not* designed to teach you fundamental marketing concepts or techniques. Rather, it illustrates a few fundamental pitfalls to avoid in your campaigns and highlights several effective systems and methods that have been tested in the new homes sales marketplace since 1978.

Signage

Consider this call.

"Hi! I'm Stephen Brown. My wife is with me. We read about your neighborhood in the paper. We've even got the little map in the ad with us, but we can't find you. Can you help us?"

"Can I help them?" thinks the agent, "You Bet!"

"Now, let's see. You're on 77 South at Big Ben's Biscuit Ranch? You're not far. Just get back on Highway 77, travel about two miles until you get to the intersection of 77 and State Road 1619. Look for a small black and white state road sign—be careful or you'll pass it. Turn right. Go about four blocks to McDonald's and turn left on the second street after McDonald's. We're on the right about a mile down the road."

Are you confused? Is the caller confused? Just think, he's in a phone booth trying to write all of this down with one hand.

If there's a cardinal rule to new home selling, it's this: If your homes can't be found, they can't be bought! Signage is the single most important ingredient. There are five types of signs to consider:

1. *Billboard Signage* is desirable for properties within an easy drive of the major traffic arteries. Billboards need to achieve three objectives:

    a. Sell community identity including name and logo

    b. Sell community theme such as:

        ■ Leisure

        ■ Golf

        ■ Waterfront

        ■ Affordability

        ■ Security

    c. Sell phone number to call for information and put address of community or travel instructions such as Exit @ 13A. Travel South. Two miles on right.

2. *Directional Signs* are excellent to draw traffic from major highways and neighborhood streets. They can be permanent or temporary. Check your area sign ordinances to confirm requirements and restrictions. Directional signs must identify the site by name or logo and show directional arrows. Keep the background dark with white letters for easy visibility day or night.

3. *Primary Entrance Signage*. Don't skimp! Remember that your homes will be partially evaluated based on the sophistication, accuracy, design and character of your signage. Area landscaping and lighting are also key ingredients to showcasing the signage.

    a. Complete entry signage *before* opening your site for visitors.

    b. Design an entry that reflects the quality/design of your community.

    c. Use high impact lettering for the site name whether choosing metal letters, wooden letters or printed/painted letters. Select an easy to read size, style and shape compatible with the community design.

4. *Onsite Directional Signs* are a *must*! They may include any or all of the following:

a. *A Welcome Sign*

b. *Directional Signs* to model, sales center, clubhouse, pools, tennis courts, private lake or any other amenity are useful in planned unit development communities that feature many types of products located on a large tract of land.

c. *Street Signs* are needed from the day you get your underground services in and have your roads prepared for ingress and egress.

d. *Model Home Signs* that identify the model by name should be mounted on the front lawn or affixed to the door itself. Be certain the name is in keeping with the community name.

e. *Amenity Signs* are excellent to position throughout the community to let the consumer know what amenities will be located where.

f. *Thank You for Coming Signs*

Don't clutter the homes or homesites with signs. Avoid placing the following in front of the home:

• Power Company Energy Saver Sign

• Lender Sign

• REALTOR® Sign

• Builder Sign

• Painter Sign

To solve the need to identify and promote each of these entities, create one sign in the site colors and mount it at a corner adjacent to several of the lots. If there are several builders in the community, have each prepare signs in accordance with community colors in a very conservative size to be ground mounted adjacent to the front corner of the driveway. Signs are the best way to attract attention to your community, so be versatile and liberal in your use of them!

Media Mania

This section focuses on marketing through the media. Encourage the builder to utilize the services of a professional marketing organization to put together an effective media campaign. The campaign should reflect frequency, the organization to be used and the cost. The builder and agent are to provide background information that identifies the source of prospects, the age, marital status and lifestyle preferences of site visitors and purchasers.

Media Marketing Proposal

Exhibit 11.2 on pages 178-180 provides samples of the type of media proposals you might expect to receive from your marketing company.

When dealing with media, remember the following truisms:

Truism #1: "Less is better" when it comes to copy, photos, color and graphics. Keep it simple for high impact. Every word, color or image must portray optimum power. Develop a succinct theme for your ad or ad campaign and use it with every word and every visual.

Truism #2: Editorial copy, even if it's only a caption under a photo or a third party endorsement, such as an article about your site in the REALTOR® section of the paper, carry far more clout than any full page ad in the world. As a new home sales specialist, build rapport with the real estate editor and seek to become an industry spokesperson whom they will call when writing articles. Invite the media to preview your site before you ever open it to the public. Roll out the red carpet. Volunteer through your Board of REALTORS® to work on the media committee for the board to further your rapport. Provide photos of major site activities with brief captions to the Real Estate editor. Encourage the editor to use them whenever fillers are needed.

The media is far too complex to discuss adequately in one chapter; it requires an entire marketing book. Media is, however, necessary to reach the masses. Balance your media through the use of radio, newspapers, area tabloids, television (particularly cable TV programming). Tailor the positioning of your ads to the buyer profile of your product, and advertise during peak seasons of the year when you have the greatest buyer interest. Media effectiveness can be evaluated by an increase in the number of site visitors and subsequent purchasers. If you see no results within 30 days, modify the ad and run it another 15 days. If there are *still* no results, pull it!

Try keeping samples of every ad that catches your eye. If it's a radio commercial, jot down the memorable part. If it's a TV commercial, make note of the memorable visual and auditory program features for future reference. This personal resource can be used when discussing future campaigns with your marketing firm.

Exhibit 11.2   Media Marketing Proposal

July—September Campaign

1. Coliseum Mall Advertising

    (12 months @ $325.00 = $3,900.00 Annual)

    3 months - July, August, September

(3 months @ $325.00)	$ 975.00
Ad Development @ $450.00	$ 450.00
Cost per quarter if the ad is changed every quarter.	$1,425.00
Cost per month	$ 475.00

2. Daily Press

    Location map with 10 lines of copy in the Open House

    Classified—Friday, Saturday, Sunday @ $550.00

    per week x 4 weeks

    Cost per month $ 2200.00

3. Full page, monthly *Homes & Land* ad

	Cost	Discount w/payment of ad
Richmond (per month)	$ 589.00	$ 529.00
Prince George County	320.00	280.00
Northern Virginia	765.00	665.00*
Hampton/Newport News	325.00	295.00
Greater Tidewater	432.00	376.00
Total cost per month	$2,431.00	$2,145.00**

*Multiple discounted issue

**This is the figure used in the total.

   Ad development for out-of-town publications

   Sizing charges of $250.00 per sizing. $750.00/quarter

Exhibit 11.2 (cont'd)   Media Marketing Proposal

---

4. Small Onsite Broker Events

    Two (2) in July @ $406.75 each $812.00/month

    July 19th and July 26th

    Two (2) in August @ $406.75 each $812.00/month

    August 23rd and August 30th

    Two (2) in September @ $406.75 $812.00/month

    Dates to be announced

5. *VA Pilot/Ledger Star*—"Home Search"

    Items are in racks by mid-afternoon Saturday—replenished

    on Wednesday; Sent to Board of REALTORS® and large real estate offices

    Full page - color $168.00*

    Offer contract discounts:

    13 week contract—$160.00*

    51 week contract—$152.00*

    5 percent payment discount

    *$100.00 per color separation.

6. Direct Mail

    3,000 pieces @ $10.75 each for mailing per month $322.50

    *July - Direct Mail Brochure

    *August - *Homes & Land* Overrun

    September - Invitations to All Day Sail Party

    (Proposed cost of invitations $1,000.00)

*Direct Mail pieces budgeted in previous marketing package of services.

**Costs of marketing per month = $3,974.50

Additional one time quarterly charge of $1,250.00 for one ad developed and two sizings of ads.

Note: NDE, Ltd. original proposal of $3,000.00 per month was for media only. Please note that your budget included $812.00 per month for events and $322.50 per month for mailing.

Exhibit 11.2 (cont'd)   **Media Marketing Proposal**

Month-at-a-Glance

August

Sunday	Monday	Tuesday	Wednesday	Thursday	Friday	Saturday
(shaded)	*(shaded)*		Homes & Land Prince George County deadline — **1**	Homes & Land Greater Tidewater distribution — **3**	Daily Press Open House directory — **4**	Daily Press Open House directory — **5**
Daily Press Open House directory — **6**	Direct mail overview — **7**	— **8**	— **9**	— **10**	Daily Press Open House directory — **11**	Daily Press Open House directory — **12**
Daily Press Open House directory — **13**	— **14**	Homes & Land Prince George County distribution — **15**	Homes & Land Greater Tidewater Copy deadline — **16**	— **17**	Daily Press Open House directory — **18**	Daily Press Open House directory — **19**
Daily Press Open House directory — **20**	— **21**	— **22**	Realtor event — **23**	— **24**	Daily Press Open House directory; Home & Land Richmond deadline — **25**	Daily Press Open House directory — **26**
Daily Press Open House directory — **27**	— **28**	Realtor event — **29**	Homes & Land Prince George County copy deadline — **30**	Homes & Land Greater Tidewater distributed — **31**	*(shaded)*	*(shaded)*

Event Planning

Events cost time, energy and dollars, so use a simple tried and true method. Review the do's and don'ts. Tailor them to your needs and enjoy your success. Exhibit 11.3 on pages 183-188 is a series of forms to be used in planning events.

What To Do

Make events memorable through . . .

- *The Invitation Process*—Develop a seasonal (Octoberfest) or prestige (white glove affair) theme and carry this out in all aspects of the event.

  - *The Design*—Design invitations that are dynamic and creative. Give them a fragrance or a touch that's special. Example: Have a fresh rose delivered with every invitation to the white glove affair. Use models dressed to reflect the theme and deliver invitations to sales meetings.

- *The Menu*—Make it special (no wine and cheese . . . Please!) It should reflect your theme.

- *The Entertainment*—Keep it a surprise! Tuck entertainers in the least likely places such as an upstairs bedroom or have them roam through the crowds; use strolling minstrels.

- *The Gifts*—"Walking Billboards" Give gifts that keep on selling your site. Consider using visors, shirts, coffee mugs, or kites, balloons and coloring books for kids to help sell the community long after the event.

- *The Follow-Up*—Mail evaluation forms to every guest to solicit their input and use as an excellent follow-up tool! See page 177 for a sample.

Timing is everything to capture agent attendance.

- *Schedule delivery* of the invitations *one* week prior to the event.

- *Schedule the event* for a Sales Meeting Day. Most cities have real estate company meetings one day each week. Have the event between 11:30 A.M. and 2:00 P.M. to capture peak attendance after the sales meeting.

- *Avoid scheduling this event* on local or state Board of REALTORS® special education days or on the same day as a major community event.

Who are the guests?

- *The REALTORS®*—They are the first sell since 80 percent of all new homes are sold by co-broke agents.

- *The VIPs*—Lenders, city officials, planning and zoning officials, elected officials and media representatives should be included.

- *The Public*—Invite the public to large, bonanza type promotions that sell large numbers of properties. (Such an event needs to be separate from a REALTOR® VIP event.)

Handle parking and traffic congestion.

- *Anticipate easy access* to and from the community for your guests. Provide traffic police.

- *Consider offsite* parking with limo support.

- *Use directional signs*, banners and clowns to help people find you.

Use a checklist with the vendors.

- You won't have to remember anything—everything is written down.

- Mail a copy of your checklist to your client to confirm that your bases are covered.

Use contracts with the vendors.

- Confirm the agreed upon fee and the terms of their service goods.

- Pay the balance due in full on the date of service or when the goods are delivered. Entertainment and food typically require deposits prior to the event. Note the following checklists and comments.

What Not To Do

- Don't conform to the average. Wine and cheese won't make your guests feel special. REALTORS® are too sophisticated to respond to average.

- Don't have small broker parties that have no focus. Brokers are busy—make the event worthwhile and a learning opportunity.

- Don't feel that all REALTORS® have to be invited. Some events don't apply to all REALTORS®. Target guests to your product and buyer type.

Exhibit 11.3   Event Planning Forms

Event Evaluation Questionnaire
(Community Name)
(Event)
Topics

		Excellent	Good	Fair	Poor
1.	Invitations				
2.	Delivery of Invitations				
3.	Luncheon Entertainment				
	Model Home Entertainment				
4.	Luncheon				
a.	Service				
b.	Presentation				
c.	Food and Beverage				
5.	Site Decorations				
6.	Personal Gift				
7.	Service Personnel				
a.	Registration Table				
b.	Food Service Personnel				
c.	Gift Presentation Personnel				

8. Did your visit to **(community)** introduce you thoroughly to the product?
    _____Yes   _____No

9. Will you bring future prospects to visit the site?_____Yes   _____No

10. How can we make your visit to our future events that are promoting new homes products more enjoyable? _____

    _____

    _____

11. Additional Comments: _____

    _____

    _____

        Name: _____

        Company Name: _____

We thank you for helping us improve.

        Sincerely,

        NANCY DAVENPORT-ENNIS and STAFF

Exhibit 11.3 (cont'd)   Event Planning Forms

ENTERTAINMENT CHECKLIST

Policy Statement: In an effort to ensure that every aspect of our event is executed on time, with full attention to detail, we are supplying the enclosed checklist. We will appreciate your cooperation in delivering your services and goods in accordance with this checklist. Late delivery or set-up will result in a penalty as described in the accompanying contract.

_____   Musical Instruments

_____   Same number of musicians as listed in contract

_____   Extension Cords

_____   Junction Box

_____   Amplifiers - if needed

_____   Band

_____   Solo Artist guitar

Set-Up Time _____   (30 minutes before event)

_____

Signature

_____

Date

Exhibit 11.3 (cont'd)   Event Planning Forms

RENTAL CHECKLIST

Policy Statement: In an effort to ensure that every aspect of our event is executed on time, with full attention to detail, we are supplying the enclosed checklist. We will appreciate your cooperation in delivering your services and goods in accordance with this checklist. Late delivery or set-up will result in a penalty as described in the accompanying contract.

Chairs:

_____ White _____

_____ Reg _____

Linens:

_____ White long _____

_____ Overlays _____

_____ Rounds _____

_____ Skirts _____

_____ Clips for skirts _____

Tables:

_____ Round _____

_____ Rectangle _____

Machines:

_____ Snow Cone _____

_____ Amplifier _____

_____ Stereo _____

_____ Speakers _____

_____ Extension cords _____

_____ Outlets _____

Tents:

_____ Small _____

_____ Large _____

Grass Carpet:

_____ Runner _____

_____ Other _____

_____ Gazebo _____

_____ Marquee _____

Set-Up Time_____   Date _____

Deadline Time _____

(30 minutes before event)

_____

Signature Special Events Coordinator

Exhibit 11.3 (cont'd)   Event Planning Forms

CATERER CHECKLIST

Policy Statement: In an effort to ensure that every aspect of our event is executed on time, with full attention to detail, we are supplying the enclosed checklist. We will appreciate your cooperation in delivering your services and goods in accordance with this checklist. Late delivery or set-up will result in a penalty as described in the accompanying contract.

_____   Food requested

_____   Beverages requested

_____   Cups

_____   Plates

_____   Dinner

_____   Dessert

_____   Knives, Forks, Spoons, Napkins

_____   Cups

_____   Glasses

_____   Serving utensils

_____   Serving dishes and bowls

_____   Dishes for leftovers after event

_____   Floral arrangement if requested

_____   Extension cords

Set-Up Time _____   Date_____

Deadline Time _____

(30 minutes before event)

_____

Signature Special Events Coordinator

Exhibit 11.3 (cont'd)   **Event Planning Forms**

MODEL AGENCY CHECKLIST

Policy Statement: In an effort to ensure that every aspect of our event is executed on time, with full attention to detail, we are supplying the enclosed checklist. We will appreciate your cooperation in delivering your services and goods in accordance with this checklist. Late delivery or set-up will result in a penalty as described in the accompanying contract.

_____   Models

_____   Male

_____   Female

_____   Costumes

Set-Up Time _____   Date _____

Deadline Time _____

(30 minutes before event) _____

_____

Signature Special Events Coordinator

Exhibit 11.3 (cont'd)   Event Planning Forms

Dear

 This letter is to confirm our agreement to have you entertain for the **(Name of Community and City)**.
 Date:
 Time:
 Location:
 Phone #:
 Fee:
 Please note that you are required to be onsite at least 30 minutes prior to starting time (at least by 10:30 A.M.). Late delivery or set-up will result in a penalty of 10 percent against the gross amount of your service.
 Also, please find a checklist enclosed. We appreciate your cooperation and ask that you please sign and return the original checklist and contract to **(Name of your Company)** in the enclosed self-addressed envelope by _____, 19_____. If you have any questions, please do not hesitate to contact me.

                                        Sincerely,

Enclosure

_____   _____
                                                Date

- Don't mail invitations just to the broker. Brokers are busy and don't need the added responsibility of getting your people to the event.

- Don't hand copies of your invitation to the secretary in the office. Copies don't make a strong statement about you. The invitation is your guest's first impression of your event.

Whether your event is for 10 or 100, with a budget of $50 or $1,000, make it memorable. Highlight your product to the visitors and make it a day—and a community—to remember. Your site and all products need to be in polished condition with the landscaping, models and printed materials completed to perfection.

Schedule a ribbon cutting by local officials to open the site event and do have the media present. Events are only as successful as your subsequent follow-up and sales—your opportunity to sell *begins* in earnest when you follow up with attendees after the event.

Brochures

When is the last time you were given a brochure that impressed you? What rang your bells and whistles? Was it the weight, the feel of the paper, the drama of the color combinations, the character of the letters, the layout of the pages, the straightforward, succinct message? Did it leave you wanting to see more or know more about the product it was selling? Your customers are impressed in the same way. A textbook-like brochure turns off the customer. Brochures that are cartoonist offend the customer. Brochures that bait with information but fail to give basic facts frustrate the customer. Brochures that visually and factually create drama do capture attention. The following do's and don'ts will pave the way for your successful brochure development.

What To Do

Your theme must reflect your buyer groups—the primary and tertiary markets. Capture the essence of these groups in photos and copywrite a lifestyle description with which they can identify. Carefully select your papers, your color schemes, your type face and your graphic and photographic support. *Make all selections based on versatility and the ability to use elements of it in future ads and handouts.*

The tone of the brochure needs to stress the emotional aspects of your community—each theme applies to specific buyer groups.

- *Privacy* appeals to singles, empty nesters and seniors.

- *Prestige product or location* appeals to move-up buyers, seniors and white collar singles.

- *Lifestyle descriptions* need to reflect the type of life in the community in photos, graphics and verbiage.

- *Luxury features* appeal to empty nesters, yuppies/move-up executives.

- *Security issues* appeal to seniors, singles, young families. Cul-de-sac features and fences are examples.

■ *Investment advantages* appeal to all groups. The tax stability of the investment and appreciation are key concerns.

Reflect specifics in an appealing manner.

■ *Floor plans* can be warmed up with furniture placements, full color or duotone treatment, shrubbery along the exterior perimeters and the naming of the floor plans. Write a statement that emotionally describes the home.

■ *Include standard features*, but describe them emotionally and categorize them with headings.

■ *Do mention "affordability"* or "attractively priced" if pricing is one of your strongest amenities. Avoid printing specific prices.

■ *Photos* speak a thousand words—let them reflect lifestyle, activities and amenities onsite.

What Not To Do

Don't begin without a community theme. Determine the number one appeal of the neighborhood and build a theme around it: Affordability, Location, Space Design, Prestige, Security. Example: Woods Run—A Neighborhood with Deer Neighbors

■ Don't be convinced that brochures sell houses—they only condition the buyer for a sale.

■ Don't bury the consumer in specifics; the following should be discussed with a professional sales associate:

– Square footage—sell volume, space arrangement, privacy, design.

– Room dimensions. It is legally disastrous to print room dimensions. If the builder misses by an inch, you're in a lawsuit!

■ Don't quote prices—quote *ranges*. Give the customer a reason to talk to you. Price sheets discourage interest. Make note of the price in your handwriting on the floor plan of your customer's choice.

■ Don't quote options with prices—prices change. Quote the options—but save the prices for personal discussion and personal notes.

■ Don't include the terms of Homeowner Association Membership. Legal issues need to be reviewed with the Sales Associate. They should be highlighted, kept in the site notebook and presented at the time a contract is authorized.

- Don't include an extensive list of standard features; this bores the buyer. Use warm headings such as energy efficiency, easy maintenance, comfort features, convenience pluses. Buyers will seek out the specific categories that interest them.

- Don't picture empty floor plans. Show furniture and plants in rooms to add warmth.

- Avoid a cluttered format. Keep it simple. Sell the top three features and benefits of the community.

Let your brochure become a silent salesperson in your absence, but don't make it an encyclopedia that puts you out of business with the buyer.

Promoting Your Builder and the Community

To succeed in marketing new homes, aggressive attention must be devoted to promoting the builder to everyone. It is appropriate to let the buyers, prospects and co-broke agents know what your builder is doing to create sales momentum and satisfied customers. Consider printing for prospects and agents a summary of the builder's marketing programs. The following summary was prepared to inform customers and co-broke agents of all that the builder was doing to *inform* and *educate* both the buying and selling marketplaces about the community. Once you review this summary, modify it for use in promoting your builders.

Exhibit 11.4 on pages 192–195 is a sample presentation of the builder's media and event promotion as discussed earlier in this chapter.

Exhibit 11.4   Promoting the Builder

HERE IS WHAT OUR BUILDER

HAS DONE TO SUPPORT

THE SALES MOMENTUM

AT HIS COMMUNITY

(Community Name)

Exhibit 11.4 (cont'd)   Promoting the Builder

He Has Produced a Videotape

_____ (Builder Name) has produced a five minute videotape that features his community and its advantages to owners and prospective purchasers. The tape can be viewed at the site, mailed to you or given to you to take home for personal viewing.

The Builder has produced 2 :30 second TV commercials to reach his buyer groups.

Ads have been placed on CABLE TV!

May 5	7:30 P.M.—8:00 P.M.	Boaters' World
May 12	7:30 P.M.—8:00 P.M.	Boaters' World
May 13	1:00 P.M.—2:30 P.M.	USTA Clay Court
May 14	3:00 P.M.—5:00 P.M.	USTA Clay Court
May 20	7:30 P.M.—8:00 P.M.	Boaters' World
May 21	2:00 P.M.—4:30 P.M.	Lafenza Cup Tennis
May 27	7:30 P.M.—8:00 P.M.	Boaters' World
May 29	12:00 P.M.—1:30 P.M.	NCAA Women's Tennis
June 2	7:30 P.M.—8:00 P.M.	Boaters' World
June 3	9:00 P.M.—2:00 P.M.	French Open Tennis
June 9	7:30 P.M.—8:00 P.M.	Boaters' World
June 16	7:30 P.M.—8:00 P.M.	Boaters' World
June 24	7:30 P.M.—8:00 P.M.	Boaters' World

Exhibit 11.4 (cont'd)   Promoting the Builder

Ads have been placed in Print Media!
PRINT SCHEDULE

Portfolio (full run)
- May 23 — Full Page
- June 6 — 1/4 Page
- June 20 — 1/4 Page

Splash
- May 12 — 1 col x 14"
- May 26 — 1 col x 14"
- June 9 — 1 col x 14"

Military Newspapers:
Soundings
- May 11 — Full Page
- May 18 — 1/4 Page (3 col x 6")
- June 8 — 1/4 Page
- June 22 — 1/4 Page
- July 6 — Full Page

The Flyer
- May 12 — Full Page
- May 26 — 1/4 Page (3 col x 6")
- June 9 — Full Page
- June 23 — 1/4 Page
- July 7 — Full Page
- July 14 — 1/4 Page

The Casement
- May 5 — Full Page
- May 19 — 1/4 Page (3 col x 6")
- June 2 — Full Page
- June 16 — 1/4 Page
- June 30 — Full Page
- July 14 — 1/4 Page

Homes & Land
- May 19 — Full Page, 4C
- June 16 — Full Page
- July 14 — Full Page

Homes
- May 15 — Full Page, B/W
- May 29
- June 12
- June 26
- July 10
- July 24

Exhibit 11.4 (cont'd)   Promoting the Builder

The builder has planned ten broker events beginning in June and lasting through August.

At the first event, 274 brokers and REALTORS® attended from Virginia Beach, Norfolk, Williamsburg and the Peninsula. Two weeks after the event, one contract has been written and accepted and one contract is being negotiated. Daily site traffic has increased by 50 percent and co-broke agents regularly show the property when working with buyers in this price range.

Sales Success

Success in sales begins with a full disclosure of your personal sales strengths and past successes (awards, designations, credentials) as well as the constant disclosure of your builder's products and services and the informational strategies he or she is using to reach the public.

Service Personnel behind the Neighborhood

To put your best foot forward with your new home purchasers, provide them with a thorough summary of all of the service related support persons who were a part of this community, their phone numbers and addresses. The list of persons and companies would include the following:

- Attorney
- Surveyor
- Engineer
- Contractors
  - Footings
  - Foundations
  - Framing
  - Roofing
  - Plumbing
  - Electrical
  - Insulation
  - Heating/Cooling Ventilation
  - Exterior finishing

— Interior finishing

— Painting

— Cabinetmaker

— Supplier of light fixtures

— Supplier of wall coverings

— Painter

— Mason

— Merchandiser or Decorator

— Advertising

— Public Relations

— Others

Hidden Values of the Neighborhood

Every neighborhood has a host of invisible special features that make it special. Examples include Little Leagues, garden clubs, babysitting co-ops, special services such as lawn care, home maintenance, alterations and security features such as Neighborhood Crime Watch.

Geographic features also make a neighborhood special and although they can be seen, they still need to be pointed out to the new purchasers. Be sure to mention babbling brooks or streams, scenic views of mountains, valleys, plains or water, and very special historic geography, such as the site of a previous civil war home that was known throughout the region.

Celebrity references should also be noted when selling your neighborhood. If the golf course is being designed by a celebrity golfer, point that out to the consumer. If well-known political, media or entertainment figures live in close proximity to your neighborhood or if they plan to build in your neighborhood, share that with your consumers. (Be certain you have the celebrities' permission to do this if they plan to live in your neighborhood.)

If the neighborhood's location makes it the créme-de-la-créme of your city due to convenience, prestige or status, promote this to everyone who visits the community. Remember, out-of-towners won't know why this location is so special unless you tell them. Your role is to promote all of the special features—even the hidden ones—of your neighborhoods.

Hidden Value of the New Home

Everyone buying a new home yearns for a *bargain*—even if their price tag is one million dollars and up. The bargain may be financial, such as builder buydown of interest rates or builder deferment of Homeowner's Association Fees for a year. It could be construction pluses such as an upgrade joist floor support system with tongue and groove, nailed and glued application of the sub flooring or future savings pluses such as optimum insulation that qualifies the home for energy saver discounts. Ask the builder to "list and describe the *strongest* selling features of your homes and community?" The following suggestions may foster creative answers:

- Energy efficiency
- Security
  - Systems
  - Gates
  - Guards
- Garage doors
- Prestige location
- Custom features
  - Special touches
  - Built-in cabinets
  - Skylights
  - Fireplaces (double faced)
  - Large rooms
  - Kitchen
  - Master bedroom
  - Master bath
  - Amenities package
- Pool
- Tennis court
- Clubhouse
- Park
- Close proximity to the above

Another method that proves extremely helpful when explaining what your homes offer that the competition doesn't involves the use of a product comparison chart. With this method, you literally compare your product to other similar and competing products in your marketplace. Areas of comparison include:

- Exterior covering
- Roof covering
- Number of bedrooms
- Arrangement of rooms
- Other features such as electronic door lock systems, laundry chutes
- Optional features such as central vacuum systems, fireplace in master suite, custom interior blinds or shutters
- Opening date of the site
- Price range
- Range of square footage
- Fireplace
- Patio/Porches
- Deck
- Garage (size, finish percentage)
- Ceilings (trundle, vaulted, cathedral)
- Windows (type, name brand)
- Heating system
- Whirlpool tub
- Ceiling fans
- Appliances

Note the attached sample comparison charts in Exhibit 11.5 on pages 199-200.

Another extremely beneficial tool is the Amenities Comparison Chart. It functions the same as the product comparison chart, but focuses on the comparison of amenities such as:

- Mountains on site
- Adjacent to a body of water: Name

Exhibit 11.5   Product Comparison

Southall Landings
June 13, 1989

	Fireplace	Patio	Deck	Garage	Ceilings	Windows	Heating System	Whirlpool Tubs	Ceiling Fans	Appliances
Southall Landings	X	X	X	X	9 Ft. Living Cathedral Vaulted	Pella	Heat Pump	X	Master Bedroom, Den	Jennaire: Range, Dshwsh, Disposal, Microwave, Refr., Trash Compactor
Windward Towers		X	Balcony		8 Ft. Living	Tecco	Electric	X		GE: Dishwasher, Disposal, Refrigerator
Salt Ponds	X		X	X	9 Ft. Living	Acroline	Natural Gas	Jacuzzi	Pre-wired but not included	Kenmore: Range, Dishwasher, Disposal,
Pine Cone Harbor	X				Cathedral Ceilings 3rd Floor	Thermo Break Insulated	Heat Pump		Master Bedroom, Den	Whirlpool: Dishwasher, Disposal
Pooles Grant	X	X	X	Car Port	Cathedral Ceilings 3rd Floor	Andersen	Heat Pump	Jacuzzi		GE: Dishwasher, Disposal, Trash Compactor
Mill Creek Landing	X	Balcony	3rd Floor Units		Cathedral Ceilings 3rd Floor	Andersen	Heat Pump		Master Bedroom, Den	Whirlpool: Dishwasher, Washer, Dryer, Refrigerator

Revised June 22, 1989

Information furnished by site agents.
Comparison prepared by NDE Impressions, Inc.

Exhibit 11.5 (cont'd)   Product Comparison

Southall Landings
June 13, 1989

	Roof Covering	Exterior	Number of Bedrooms	Arrangment of Rooms	Other	Options	Opening date of Site	Price Range	Range of Square Ft.
Southall Landings	Shingle	Dryvit Brick	2,3	Dining, Living, Kitchen, Baths, Bedrooms	Electronic Door Lock with Speaker System, Cable Hook-Up, Smoke Detectors	Central Vacum System, Fireplace in Master Bedroom	September, 1988	122,5 - 237,5+	1524-2683 Sq. Ft.
Windward Towers	Shingle	Stucco	1,2,3	Dining, Living, Kitchen, Baths, Bedrooms	Cable Hook-Up, Trash Chute, Smoke Detectors		August, 1985	High 70's-250,8	800-1400 Sq. Ft.
Salt Ponds	Shingle/Asphalt	Not maintenance free—Cedar/Stucco Siding	2,3	Dining, Formal Living, Kitchen, Baths, Bedrooms	Smoke Detectors, Cable Hook-Up, Security Monitoring	Blinds, Stove, Refrigerator	June, 1989	109,5 - 157,5	1244-1804 Sq. Ft.
Pine Cone Harbor	Fiberglass Shingle	Vinyl Siding	2,3	Dining, Living, Kitchen, Baths, Bedrooms	Cable Hook-Up, Smoke Detectors	Refrigerator, Stove, Microwave Oven, Ceiling Fans	May, 1987	Mid 70's-106,9	1235-1435 Sq. Ft.
Pooles Grant	Cedar Shingle	Brick	2,3	Kitchen, Living-Dining Combination	Security Gate, Telephone Hook-Up in Kitchen, Living, Master Bedroom, Bath	Microwave Oven, Trash Compactor, Grill	March, 1989	197,9 - 247,00	1409-1827 Sq. Ft.
Mill Creek Landing	Shingle	Vinyl Siding	2,3	Living-Dining Combination, Bedrooms, Bath	Cable Hook-Up, Smoke Detectors	Ceiling Fans, Upgraded Carpet, Mirrors in Living Area	May, 1989	89,9 - 85,9	1300-1350 Sq. Ft.

Information furnished by site agents.
Comparison prepared by NDE Impressions, Inc.

Revised June 22, 1989

- Racquetball court (indoor/outdoor)

- Tennis courts

- Pool

- Boat slips

- Clubhouse

- Jogging, walking, biking paths

- Weight/exercise room

- Hot tubs

- Sauna

- Locker with shower rooms

- Other

See Exhibit 11.6 on page 202 for an amenity comparison chart.

As a new homes specialist, maintain the highest level of visibility for your community and your builder by constantly promoting what's not obvious. Move away from selling rooms, sticks and bricks and depart from the emotional sell of the '80s. Today's consumers are practical and demand facts about their prospective new home. Surprise your buyers . . . give them the obvious facts and immediately move them into the realm of hidden home and neighborhood values as well as comparison charts of products and amenities. Put them in the driver's seat of the decision making process after you've armed them with the information to motivate a thoroughly informed and confident decision. The result will be a satisfied purchaser and a well-respected new homes agent. There are no shortcuts to that type of success. It's the route to excellence!

Exhibit 11.6   Amenities Comparison

Southall Landings
June 13, 1989

	Body of Water	Raquetball Courts	Tennis Courts	Pool	Boat Slips	Clubhouse	Jogging Trails	Weight/Exercise Room	Hot Tub	Sauna	Locker Room with Showers	Other Amenities
Southall Landings	Chesapeake Bay	Two inside, one outside	2	2	X	X	X	X	X	X	X	Lounge affairs 150-175
Windward Towers	James River		2	X	Fee paid to city of Newport News	X		X		X	X	Meeting Rooms, Undergr Parking
Salt Ponds	Salt Ponds			Summer 1990	Fee: $58/mnth	Summer 1990						
Pine Cone Harbor	Hampton River			X	Purchase: 5800 63,00	X		X				
Pooles Grant	Hampton River		1	X	Purchase: 12.500 30,000	X						

Information furnished by site agents.
Comparison prepared by NDE Impressions, Inc.

Revised June 22, 1989

12

Epilogue: Knowing Where To Tap

The Old Boilermaker

Once upon a time, a boilermaker was hired to fix a huge steamship boiler system. After listening to the engineer's description of the problems and asking a few questions, he went to the boiler room.

He looked at the maze of twisting pipes, listened to the thump of the boiler and the hiss of escaping steam for a few minutes and felt some pipes with his hand. Humming softly to himself, he reached into his overalls, took out a small hammer and tapped a bright red valve once.

Immediately the entire system began working perfectly, and the boilermaker went home. When the steamship owner received a bill for $1,000, he complained that the boilermaker had only been in the engine room for ten minutes and requested an itemized bill. It soon came in the mail:

For tapping with the hammer	$ .50
For knowing where to tap	<u>999.50</u>
TOTAL	$1,000.00

This old story might help you understand your role in representing your builder's products in today's marketplace as well as the goals of this book. In the business of new home sales, you must know "where to tap" to find qualified prospects, convert prospects to purchasers and continually work with the builder to mutually position your product in a leading edge position in the marketplace. You must also use your "little red hammer"— a combination of your experience, market research, and real estate knowledge—to develop and deliver effective results to the builder.

There are many opportunities in life to reach for new horizons—and every opportunity is surrounded by an abundance of challenges. Any challenge worth meeting enhances character, and this is especially true if you are involved in new home sales. Our industry is dramatically impacted by:

- the economy;

- the employment stability of our nation;

- the strength of our international marketplaces;

- buyer attitudes;

- media messages;

and a thousand other variables. The state-of-the-art sales and skills available in our industry form the foundation upon which to build a successful career in new home sales. We must also practice the standards of historic sales excellence such as prospecting, qualifying, demonstrating and closing if we are to build a stable base of sales success.

This book is a combination of the two. It is my gift of thirteen years of experience as a builder, sales trainer, new home consultant and national speaker to highlight for you the systems that repeatedly have proven effective in the marketplaces across America where I've had the opportunity to serve. Crystallize from this text the materials that will help you daily and maintain this book for easy reference when dealing with an isolated challenge. Last, but not least, know that in overcoming your new home sales challenges, you are developing new character that will serve you well in capturing new opportunities. My very best wishes to you on your journey of opportunities!

Index